ENTREPRENEURSHIP
Bilingual Teaching Case

创业学
双语教学案例

主　编　王　健　陈士慧
副主编　蒋　鑫　国维潇

北京大学出版社
PEKING UNIVERSITY PRESS

内 容 简 介

创业学是一门理论联系实际，实践性、运用性较强的课程。全书共设计了 14 个案例来展现不同企业的创业实践，揭示创业理论在实际中的运用，实现以创业实践学习创业理论，以创业理论洞悉创业实践的教学目的。通过对案例的学习，读者可以了解和掌握创业学的相关理论知识，获得有关如何有效开展创业活动的实践指引。

本书主要作为高校开展创业学教育的教材及来华留学生"创业学"课程的配套教材，也适合作为企业管理培训用书和自学参考书。

图书在版编目（CIP）数据

创业学：双语教学案例 / 王健，陈士慧主编. —北京：北京大学出版社，2023.9
高等院校经济管理类专业"互联网+"创新规划教材
ISBN 978-7-301-33637-3

Ⅰ.①创… Ⅱ.①王… ②陈… Ⅲ.①创业—双语教学—教案（教育）—高等学校 Ⅳ.① F241.4

中国版本图书馆 CIP 数据核字（2022）第 233002 号

书　　　名	创业学：双语教学案例 CHUANGYEXUE: SHUANGYU JIAOXUE ANLI
著作责任者	王　健　陈士慧　主编
策 划 编 辑	李娉婷
责 任 编 辑	张　越　陶鹏旭
标 准 书 号	ISBN 978-7-301-33637-3
出 版 发 行	北京大学出版社
地　　　址	北京市海淀区成府路 205 号　100871
网　　　址	http://www.pup.cn　　新浪微博：@ 北京大学出版社
电 子 邮 箱	编辑部 pup6@pup.cn　　总编室 zpup@pup.cn
电　　　话	邮购部 010-62752015　发行部 010-62750672　编辑部 010-62750667
印 刷 者	北京市科星印刷有限责任公司
经 销 者	新华书店
	787 毫米 ×1092 毫米　16 开本　13.25 印张　191 千字 2023 年 9 月第 1 版　2023 年 9 月第 1 次印刷
定　　　价	45.00 元

未经许可，不得以任何方式复制或抄袭本书之部分或全部内容。

版权所有，侵权必究

举报电话：010-62752024　电子信箱：fd@pup.pku.edu.cn
图书如有印装质量问题，请与出版部联系，电话：010-62756370

前　言

当前，我国涌现出一批具有国际影响力的知名企业和创业者，吸引着越来越多的国外学生来华学习。宁波大学作为较早从事国际化课程教学的中国院校，很早就计划编写一部案例教材，以满足"创业学"双语或全英文教学的配套需要。

本教材适合用于高等院校工商管理类本科生及来华留学生"创业学"课程的配套教材，也适合作为企业管理培训用书和自学参考书。

本教材选取14个中国本土创业案例来阐明创业基本理论知识，可以让来华留学生了解我国企业的创业实践。本教材涵盖了创业学的主要知识点。案例1主要研究的是创业类型、创业与创新的区别；案例2研究的是认知创业准备、创业思维对创业的重要性；案例3研究的是创业者素质与能力；案例4用于学习市场导向与创业；案例5用于学习创业团队领导者；案例6研究的是创业团队冲突与管理；案例7研究的是外部环境对创业机会识别的影响；案例8研究的是机会导向与创业营销；案例9研究的是资源拼凑；案例10研究的是Timmons创业要素模型；案例11研究的是商业模式要素；案例12研究的是商业模式画布与商业模式创新；案例13研究的是社会创业；案例14研究的是家族创业。每个案例都包括知识点、案例目的、案例正文、思考题与分析提示。

本教材的编写与出版历时两年有余，具体分工如下：案例1～13由宁波大学商学院王健编写；案例14由宁波大学商学院陈士慧编写；中共云南省委党校（云南行政学院）蒋鑫博士负责本教材部分案例的翻译及校对工作。全书由王健统稿。

本教材的顺利出版，得益于宁波大学工商管理国际化专业建设项目的支持。感谢北京大学出版社耐心细致的编辑工作。

由于编写者水平有限，本教材如有不足之处，恳请同行、读者批评指正！

王健

宁波大学商学院

Preface

Currently, China has seen the emergence of a number of internationally influential renowned companies and entrepreneurs, attracting an increasing number of foreign students to study in China. As one of the Chinese universities that started early with international curriculum teaching, Ningbo University had long planned to compile a case study textbook to meet the needs of bilingual or fully English-taught "Entrepreneurship Studies" courses.

This textbook is suitable for undergraduate students majoring in business administration in higher education institutions and as a supporting textbook for the "Entrepreneurship Studies" course for international students studying in China. It is also suitable for enterprise management training and self-study reference.

This textbook selects 14 Chinese domestic entrepreneurship cases to illustrate basic theoretical knowledge in entrepreneurship, allowing international students to understand China's entrepreneurial practices. The textbook covers the main knowledge points of entrepreneurship. Case 1 mainly explores the types of entrepreneurship and the difference between entrepreneurship and innovation; Case 2 focuses on the importance of cognitive entrepreneurial preparation and entrepreneurial thinking; Case 3 examines the qualities and abilities of entrepreneurs; Case 4 is used to study market orientation and entrepreneurship; Case 5 is used to study entrepreneurial team leadership; Case 6 focuses on entrepreneurial team conflicts and management; Case 7 explores the impact of the external environment on entrepreneurial opportunity identification; Case 8 investigates opportunity orientation and entrepreneurial marketing; Case 9 examines the principles of stakeholder and resource integration; Case 10 studies resource acquisition; Case 10 examines the Timmons Entrepreneurship Framework; Case 11 explores business model elements; Case 12 focuses on the business model canvas and business model innovation; Case 13 explores social entrepreneurship; Case 14 studies family entrepreneurship. Each case includes knowledge points, case objectives, case content, discussion questions, and analysis prompts.

It took more than two years to prepare and publish this textbook. Cases 1~13 were compiled by Wang Jian of the Business School Of Ningbo University; Case 14 was compiled by Shihui Chen of the Business School Of Ningbo University; Dr. Xin Jiang of the Party School of the Yunnan Committee of the CPC (Yunnan Academy of Governance) was responsible for translating and proofreading some of the cases in this textbook. This book was finalized by Wang Jian.

The successful publication of this textbook is due to the support of the Internationalization of Business Administration Program at Ningbo University. We are grateful to Peking University Press for their patience and meticulous editing efforts.

Due to the limited expertise of the authors, any deficiencies in this textbook are subject to criticism and correction from colleagues and readers.

Wang Jian

Business School of Ningbo University

October 16, 2022

目　录

案例 1　淘宝、拼多多与宁大云创小镇 1

案例 2　上海海庭环境工程有限公司的创业 5

案例 3　创业故事三则 11

案例 4　D 公司的失败 17

案例 5　俞敏洪的早期创业团队 23

案例 6　成江药业：创始人之间的裂痕如何修复？ 29

案例 7　张朝阳的早期创业历程 35

案例 8　E 公司的失败 41

案例 9　实用的"修补术" 45

案例 10　朗明科技的 AI 创业之路 51

案例 11　叮咚买菜的商业模式 59

案例 12　悦管家的商业模式创新之路 67

案例 13　用社会创业实现精准扶贫：龙游飞鸡 77

案例 14　创业传承：海伦钢琴 85

Case 1	Taobao, Pinduoduo, and Ningda Yunchuang Town	93
Case 2	The Entrepreneurship of Shanghai Haiting Environmental Engineering Co., Ltd.	99
Case 3	Three Entrepreneurship Stories	107
Case 4	The Failure of Company D	115
Case 5	Yu Minhong's Early-stage Entrepreneurial Team	121
Case 6	Chengjiang Pharmaceuticals: How to Repair the Rift Between Founders?	127
Case 7	Zhang Chaoyang's Early Entrepreneurial Journey	135
Case 8	The Failure of Company E	141
Case 9	A Practical "Fix"	147
Case 10	The Entrepreneurial Journey of Langming Technology in AI	153
Case 11	Dingdong's Business Model	163
Case 12	The Business Model Innovation of Yue-Life	173
Case 13	Achieving Precise Poverty Alleviation through Social Entrepreneurship: Longyou Free-range Chicken	185
Case 14	Inheritance of Entrepreneurship: Hailun Piano	195

案例 1

淘宝、拼多多与宁大云创小镇

知识点：

创业类型、创业逻辑、创业与创新。

案例目的：

通过淘宝网、拼多多和宁大云创三个案例的简单介绍，使学生掌握创业类型和创业逻辑，理解创业与创新的区别与联系。

案例正文：

淘宝网

淘宝是深受中国消费者欢迎的网购平台，拥有近5亿的注册用户，每天有超过6000万的固定访客，每天的在线商品数已经超过了8亿件，平均每分钟售出4.8万件商品。

2003年，在大众对网购和互联网的认识还比较有限的时候，马云就创办了淘宝，在国内进行C2C模式的探索。2007年，淘宝成为亚洲最大的零售网站，全年成交额突破400亿元，成为中国第二大综合卖场。当下，淘宝已从单一的C2C模式转变为包括C2C、团购、分销、拍卖等多种电子商务模式在内的综合性零售商圈，成为世界范围的电子商务交易平台之一。

拼多多

拼多多是专注于C2M拼团购物的第三方社交电商平台，成立于2015年9月。用户通过发起和朋友、家人等的拼团，可以以更低的价格购买商品。该平台旨在凝聚更多人的力量，使人们体会更多的实惠和乐趣。基于沟通分享而形成的社交理念，构成了拼多多独特的新社交电商思维。

2019年，拼多多入选2019中国品牌强国盛典榜样100品牌。2020年，拼多多名列2020福布斯全球企业2000强榜第1649位。在淘宝和京东的夹缝中，拼多多实现了强势成长，已形成了"万物皆可拼多多"的现状。

宁大云创小镇

宁波大学云创 1986 青年小镇（以下简称云创小镇），原为宁波大学东门商业街，于 2016 年 10 月 1 日开业。云创小镇聚集了餐饮、零售、休闲、教育等业态，涉及创业、文化交流、生活中心。云创小镇用旅游、文化、艺术休闲、美食、潮流娱乐、创客公寓等社群元素构成了丰富多样的业态组合，缔造出一个自成生态体系的青年社区。

当前，云创小镇的品牌有星巴克、肯德基、铁酱披萨、汤岛涮、大煲口福、六本木日料、回力、醉网咖、四合网苑、宝岛眼镜、CGV 大光明眼镜、柏家、罗森、欧文、一点点等。

案例思考题：

1. 你认为马云的创业属于机会型创业还是生存型创业？云创小镇的各个店铺，又属于哪种创业类型？

2. 马云创建淘宝采用的是因果逻辑还是效果逻辑？

3. 无论是淘宝、拼多多还是云创小镇，都聚集了大量商铺，请你从创新性上对它们进行评价，并说明创业与创新的关系。

分析提示：

1. 创业类型多种多样，其中生存型创业和机会型创业是我国两种常见的创业类型。生存型创业的动机是创业者没有其他选择，只能通过创业活动来解决其所面临的困难；而机会型创业的动机是创业者有抓住现有机会并实现价值的强烈愿望。

2. 因果逻辑和效果逻辑是创业中常使用的创业逻辑。因果逻辑以目标为导向，效果逻辑则以手段为导向。

3. 创业不等于创新，创新也并不一定会导致创业，但基于创新的创业往往更易获得成功。淘宝的创业更具创新性，而拼多多与云创小镇的整体创新性并不强，虽然三者都是创业活动，但是在创新性上各不相同。

案例 2

上海海庭环境工程有限公司的创业

知识点：

创业准备、创业技能、创业团队、创业思维。

案例目的：

本案例通过对大学生创业案例的分析，让学生了解大学生在创业过程中所面临的普遍问题和创业中的主要决策，让学生认识到创业准备的重要性。

案例正文：

张选军于1994年考入湖南大学，学习化工工业。本科毕业后，他先后进入世通广州分公司、东莞茂林电子有限公司工作。在工作中，张选军认识到自己在专业知识、管理技能等方面存在很多不足，于是决定辞职考研。2001年，他进入湘潭大学攻读环境工程硕士学位，之后进入同济大学攻读环境科学专业博士学位。

读博期间，张选军一边从事学术研究，一边积累实践经验。他先后在上海科域水处理技术有限公司和上海万泓环境科技有限公司担任项目经理与技术顾问。2007年5月，张选军开始创业，创立上海海庭环境工程有限公司。

实际上，张选军创业的想法由来已久，在大学期间他就开始积极参与社会实践活动，积累实践和工作经验，如做商场促销员、公司业务员等。这些实践使张选军领悟到了执行力的重要性，他开始组建自己的团队去实施较小的创业项目，如出售新生儿生活用品，三天净赚了6000元。后来他又陆续抓住了一些市场机遇，如出售二手自行车、摩托车、数码产品，代理信用卡、SIM卡等。本科毕业后，张选军选择去公司上班主要是基于三个方面的考虑：首先，大学期间从事的商业活动和真正的创业相比还存在很大的差距；其次，刚毕业时他的风险承受能力较弱；最后，工作能积累一些经验和人脉，为日后的创业奠定基础。

2005年，张选军的博士研究课题成为上海市科学技术委员会科研计划项目

"城镇污水厌氧处理新技术及数学模型研究"的核心研究内容，并得到了国家"十五""十一五"科技攻关计划项目的支持。在导师的指导下，张选军和他的课题组成员们经过一年多的努力，终于取得了技术性突破，研制出新型外循环厌氧反应器，并申请了国家专利。该反应器在污水处理方面具有很多优势，如结构简单、低能耗、多种污染物一体化处理、水质达标、管理简便等。

随后，新型外循环厌氧反应器应用在江苏多家废水处理厂。由于其表现优异，获得企业的一致好评。课题组与昆山和常州的两家公司达成设备推广的初步意向。在导师的大力支持下，2007 年 5 月，张选军成立了上海海庭环境工程有限公司（以下简称海庭）。张选军获得了同济大学大学生创业基金的赞助（20 万元）和导师的借款（20 万元），课题组成员刘洪波也加入团队之中。2007 年，海庭正式开始运营。

创业伊始，张选军遇到了许多困难。海庭在成立的最初半年里没有接到一单业务，处于纯粹的"烧钱"阶段，因此筹集的资金很快就用了一半。于是，张选军开始寻求经营理念上的转变，要求公司全体成员都去跑市场。接着，张选军改变了经营策略，公司不仅推广自己的产品，也代理其他产品，同时提供技术咨询服务。通过经营理念和经营策略的改变，公司逐渐有了起色，承接了大大小小的业务，也和客户建立了合作关系。

度过了艰难的生存期后，海庭步入了快速发展的通道：一方面继续扩大与各种技术型公司的合作，共同承接项目，在技术和产品上互相支持和补充；另一方面努力寻找机会推广核心产品，和市场型公司合作，采用销售代理的方式进行业务拓展。这降低了海庭的运营成本和运营风险，使总体营业额快速增长。随着业务的不断开展，海庭知名度不断提升，为日后海庭的发展奠定了良好基础。2009 年海庭销售额高达 3500 万元，比 2008 年增加了 2600 万元。

制约海庭快速发展的一个因素是缺乏职业的管理人员。在海庭成立之初，业务还是以小项目为主，而且全年的营业额也比较低，问题还不明显。但是，海庭在步入快速发展阶段后，这个问题就突显出来了。例如，项目金额比较大的业务，一般都是采用分期付款的方式进行支付，而如何设置分期付款的日期和平衡月度财务报表就是非常重要的问题。由于公司缺乏懂财务管理的人才，常常出现大量项目款在同一个月入账的情况，导致该月缴纳了大量的税费，而其他月份却没有收入或者收入很少。而且随着业务量、销售额、公司员工的不断增加，自由随意的管理方式已经不能适应海庭快速发展的需要。在运营初期对科学管理的认识不足，导致海庭在运营中遭受了许多损失。

制约海庭快速发展的另一个因素是资金。海庭的年销售额虽然已达千万级别，但是实际上可自由支配的现金却十分有限。随着海庭项目金额的增大，在项目运作阶段，需要垫付的资金也越来越多。张选军想过很多解决资金问题的办法，但都不理想。因为海庭没有可以抵押的东西，又找不到合适的人来担保贷款，所以不能向银行贷款。而私人的短期贷款，利率太高，风险太大。在当时的政策环境下，海庭也很难申请下来项目基金。因为海庭绝大多数的销售额来源于传统型业务，而核心产品的销售情况却不甚理想，所以风险投资公司也不愿意冒险。寻找不到足够的资金支持，海庭只能和其他大公司合作，共同承接金额较大的项目。但是，合作意味着利润的下降，公司资产也就很难得到快速的增长。

海庭的发展在很大程度上依赖其他公司。一方面，海庭的产品线比较单一、服务范围有限，很多项目需和其他公司共同运作。另一方面，海庭因缺乏行业内的相关资质，有些项目必须挂靠到其他公司，自身暂时还不具备独立运作的条件。此外，海庭主要以技术、产品和服务输出为主，采用和其他公司合作、实施销售代理的方式进行业务拓展，缺少自有市场拓展团队，所以很难控制每年的销售业绩，难以有计划、有步骤地扩大市场。

（资料来源：根据网络资料整理）

案例思考题：

1. 你认为大学生创业成功的关键因素有哪些？
2. 张选军为什么能在创业初期带领海庭快速发展？为什么后来又会遇到诸多问题？
3. 海庭在发展中遇到的问题是否不可避免？应如何防患于未然？

分析提示：

1. 创业经常面临着失败，因而在创业前需要做好诸多准备，如知识、技能、实践等。由于大学生并无太多社会经历，其创业行为往往具有很强的冲动性，常常忽略创业前的准备、市场调查、政策法律等。

2. 创业准备对早期创业成功具有重要影响，但是随着企业的发展壮大，其面临的内外环境也变得复杂，创业者早期的创业储备也就不足以支撑企业的发展。

3. 因为创业会面临诸多问题，如资金短缺、团队冲突等，所以创业者应具有利用不确定性的环境创造商机的思维方式。例如，创业者要进行不断的创业学习，注重团队的组建、组织的建立、快速行动、迭代试错，尽快寻找到可行的商业模式。

案例 3

创业故事三则

知识点：

创业者素质、创业者是天生还是后天培养的、创业准备。

案例目的：

创业是一条艰难的路。如果只靠激情创业而没有准备，那么这条路就是一条不归路。因此，本案例的设计具有启发性和开放性，主要是启发学生思考：①创业需要做哪些准备；②自测是否适合创业。

案例正文：

阿文的大衣橱

渴望拥有一个大衣橱，里面装满漂亮衣服，并与姐妹分享对美的感受，这是一个"80后"女生阿文创业的初衷。阿文5年前从高校毕业以后，一直从事着与自己专业相关的设计工作，与多数白领一样过着朝九晚五的生活。但那个一直以来关于大衣橱的梦想促使她走出了创业的第一步。

在服装店开张前，阿文除了懂得挑选衣服外，对经营一无所知。无论从店面装修风格到待客之道，还是衣服的定价，这些她都要从零开始学起。阿文认为刚开始创业比较难，很多经营的小细节都要靠自己摸索积累。例如，考虑到市场本身的因素和传播效果，阿文喜欢的那些店名，最后一个都没有用上。

阿文很庆幸开店以来，没有出现大差错，也没有和顾客发生不愉快的纠纷。她认为这可能是因为她在背后花了很多时间，容易出错的细节都注意到了。阿文店里的每件衣服都是她精心挑选的，她觉得看到这些漂亮的衣服穿到合适的人身上是件幸福的事情。时至今日，阿文还是一边做自己的设计工作，一边兼顾服装店的经营，她更愿意把这个地方看作和志同道合的人交流的场所。

关于创业，阿文认为身边很多人都有一个创业的梦想，却因为各种原因而迟迟没有走出第一步。

嘉嘉的桌游店

大学毕业后就有创业打算的嘉嘉，直到2009年偶然接触了一款桌面游戏（以下简称桌游）"三国杀"，才开启了他的创业之门。

当时"三国杀"还未风行，桌游也不太出名。嘉嘉当时就想，桌游对环境设备要求简单，不仅绿色健康，而且能增进朋友间的沟通交流，的确是不错的游戏。

后来他才了解到桌游在欧美已经流行了几十年，而在国内才刚开始兴起，于是他和合伙人选择了桌游店作为自己创业的"第一站"。一方面是因为资金不充裕，另一方面是因为他们当时没有做市场调查，对桌游能否被本地消费群体所接受，心里没底。

2009年7月，嘉嘉开始筹备开店。他去大城市的同类店参观学习，找桌游的进货渠道，学习一些大型桌游的玩法，以及设计收费经营模式。两个月后，桌游店正式开张。

刚开始客流源源不断，超出了嘉嘉的预料。但很快他就发现店内存在很多问题，如隔音差导致顾客之间互相干扰，人手不足导致服务质量差，收费昂贵让不少人望而却步，等等。后来，嘉嘉及其合伙人决定增加人手，重新制订收费模式，桌游店逐渐拥有了一批固定客户。

孟炎创业7个月

孟炎在大学学的是企业管理，毕业后在一家销售轴承的公司工作了一年。因为一直在跑市场，与客户打交道，孟炎很快掌握了这方面的知识和技巧，开始渴望能够创业。

他偶然得知同学小谢家中有人从事机械轴承销售，收入颇丰。并且小谢也有相关的工作经历，有一些客户资源。孟炎决定和小谢一起创业。孟炎和小谢的创业目的很明确：一是给将来打基础，二是多赚点钱。但是，他们在如何运作、目前的市场前景、这个行业的特点以及产品的性能等方面都不是行家。

2002年4月，为了创业，孟炎借了5万元，小谢借了3万多元。之后的两个多月时间里，孟炎和小谢搬到了公司住。他们白天把报价单等资料装入发给各个企业的信封中。上万封信发出去后，没有等来一个业务咨询的电话，却等来了天天从邮局退回的信件。但两人并没有灰心。2002年8月，两人开始到各个机械设备展览会现场、轴承展览会现场，向往来客商递送资料，与厂商联络。这种方法让他们收集了几百张中间商的名片，包括国内的和国外的订货商。两人对这种情况感到兴奋，他们觉得前景越来越光明。

他们把收集到的名片输入电脑，做成数据库。随着展会的后续效应，每天都有十几个客户打来电话或前来洽谈业务。一个多月后，孟炎察觉到事情有些不对劲，虽然每天都有客户来咨询，但是很少有后续。孟炎他们着急起来，专门去向一些业内人士请教。业内人士认为，机械轴承这个行业的情况很复杂，发展到现在，国内外厂商和供应商之间的关系相对稳定。因此，产品质量好、价格低未必能争取到客户。

孟炎想变被动为主动，通过上门洽谈增加与客户的直接沟通。他动员了所有的同学、朋友、家人，帮助他寻找相关企业的熟人，然而收效甚微。孟炎决定招几个业务员，并且草拟了一份销售计划。这意味着每月至少增加2000~3000元的支出。

业务员招来两个多月后，公司仍然没赚到钱，孟炎更着急了。国庆节前夕，孟炎接到了第一单生意，合同金额为7万多元，利润只有4000多元。公司又陆续签了几笔小单子，赚了不到1万元。随后，公司的业务有了起色，建立了良好的口碑，客户越来越多。虽然订单都很小，但是利润也勉强够他们每月的开支。

但是，暂时的成功并不能掩盖公司在制度方面，以及孟炎在创业方面的欠缺。公司组织不健全、构架不合理的问题原本就非常突出，加上账目混乱、员工工作秩序混乱，很快麻烦就来了。业务员为了争客户明争暗斗，互相拆台。孟炎起初并未加以重视，没想到事态逐渐恶化：一个业务员为了抢订单，竟然与厂家私下交易。当供货出现问题，厂家找孟炎要求赔偿时，那个业务员却早就走了。为了公司的声誉，孟炎做出了一定的赔偿，两个月的利润没有了。更严重的是，对于公司业务员之间的你争我夺，业内很快人尽皆知。厂家对公司产生了疑虑，公司的业务再次陷入僵局。

2002年11月，小谢提出散伙，并且带走了客户的资料。孟炎的生意彻底陷入绝境。刚起航的船，就这样触礁搁浅了。孟炎总结，当初应该先在外贸公司工作两三年，积累一定的经验和客户资源，后面创业就不会这么被动。

（资料来源：根据网络资料整理）

案例思考题：

1. 基于上述3个案例，你认为创业者一般应具备哪些方面的素质和能力？
2. 你认为创业要做好哪些方面的准备？

分析提示：

1. 阿文的案例告诉我们，创业要有对梦想的冲动，要有恒心和勇气；嘉嘉的案例告诉我们，创业前的市场调查很重要；孟炎的案例告诉我们，只有创业激情而不具备相应的能力是无法成功的。创业者一般应具有激情、警觉性、冒险性、创新性等特质。

2. 创业是一条艰辛的路，如果你在没有准备的前提下，只靠激情创业，那么这条路就是一条不归之路。创业前应做好以下方面的准备：人员、资金、市场调查、知识与经验积累等。

案例 4

D 公司的失败

知识点：

创业团队的组建、创业公司的特点、创业公司的员工管理、精益创业、市场化的创业者。

案例目的：

创业团队对创业成功起着重要作用。本案例可用于：①评估和分析创业团队的组成，以及如何有效实现团队的互补性；②让学生注意到创业中经常面临的一个导致失败的问题，即创业与市场的分离；③使学生进一步了解精益创业的相关内容，重点掌握精益创业的思想。

案例正文：

D公司创立于2008年，其主要业务是帮助软件开发者使用云服务，以更合理的方式"测试"他们的代码。王明和赵涛是D公司的联合创始人，两人结识于高中，并在高中毕业前就已创立了一家网络公司。D公司于2010年破产。D公司在破产声明中指出，尽管云技术工具改变了软件开发者的生活，但没能创造足够的收入来维持公司的运营。

赵涛认为D公司失败的原因主要集中在创始团队构成、团队沟通和产品开发三个方面。

关于创始团队，王明和赵涛都是工程师。虽然拥有一个热爱公司的伙伴是优势，但是两人都没有对做生意产生兴趣或者投入大量精力，更没有考虑测量商业指标，如顾客数量或分销渠道的开发程度等。

关于沟通，D公司创建于北京市，支持员工远程工作。D公司的第一次关键招募工作是在上海进行的，员工不需要来公司总部。王明和赵涛认为允许团队成员远程工作可以使分歧降到最低，这样能够使代码编写过程更高效。令人遗憾的是，实现这些目标远比预期的要困难。在不同的地区同时处理薪金和福利是个很大的难题。此外，结对编程很难通过远程工作的方式完成。

关于产品开发，赵涛认为 D 公司应该在顾客开发和寻找最简可行性产品上花费更多的时间。最简可行性产品是精益创业的重要组成部分，通常由早期用户进行测试，其理念是避免在产品中加入顾客不需要或不想要的额外功能。但实际上，D 公司只对第一款产品做了最小化测试，之后就专注于开发新产品，忽略了与潜在用户的交流。因此，D 公司的产品从未真正满足过市场需求。

回顾往事，两位创始人认为 D 公司应该更快地部署个人产品，并更多地听取顾客关于定价、市场规模和技术性挑战的反馈。他们最终意识到市场太小、产品价格太低以至于根本不能维持公司的运营。

（资料来源：改编自巴林杰，爱尔兰. 创业管理：成功创建新企业［M］. 薛红志，等译. 机械工业出版社，2017）

案例思考题：

1. 拥有商业导向合伙人会给 D 公司带来优势吗？如果两个商人一起创立一家技术导向型公司，你认为拥有商业导向合伙人还是优势吗？或者说应该雇用技术导向人才吗？

2. 远程工作这一形式是否适合初创企业？谈谈你的看法。

3. 很多具有技术背景的创业者更像一位工程师，他们喜欢发明新东西，而忽视顾客的需求，他们不会从顾客的角度、从价值创造的角度创新。结合本案例，谈谈如何解决这一问题。

分析提示：

1. 创业团队在组建时，需要对成员进行评估，要注重团队成员的相似性与互补性。在知识及技能上要注重互补性，在个人特质上则要注重相似性。

2. 虽然远程工作现在比较流行，但不太适宜具有自身特殊性的初创企业。初创企业的组织结构、组织文化及员工关系都具有较高的不稳定性，而远程工作不利于初创企业产生向心力。

3.喜欢创造的发明家并不一定是一个好的创业者，因为创业者要具有市场思维，注重创业与市场的联系。精益创业是一种利用最简可行性产品，不断测试和迭代的创业方式。通过这种方式，创业者可以紧密关联市场，了解市场动态，从顾客的角度进行创新。

案例 5

俞敏洪的早期创业团队

知识点：

创业团队组建、创业型领导特征。

案例目的：

本案例让学生：①了解创业型领导的重要性和特殊性，评价创业型领导；②深入思考如何组建创业团队。

案例正文：

新东方在创办之前，北京已经有三四所同类学校。参加新东方培训的主要是以出国留学为目的的学生。随着人们在工作、学习、晋升等方面对英语的要求越来越多样化以及出国热的兴起，当时国内掀起了学习英语的热潮，越来越多的优秀教师加入英语培训这个行业。如何先人一步，取得自己的竞争优势，把新东方做大、做强？俞敏洪认为英语培训行业必须要具备一流的师资。

培训学校普遍做不大是因为对个别讲师过分倚重。所以，俞敏洪需要找到合作伙伴，帮他把控英语培训各个环节的质量。而这样的人不仅要有过硬的专业知识和能力，更要和俞敏洪有共同的办学理念。他首先想到的是远在美国的王强和在加拿大的徐小平等人。这些人不仅符合业务拓展的要求，更重要的是，他们作为俞敏洪的同学、好友，与俞敏洪在思想上有着一定的共性，这样的合作也会更坚固和长久。

就在这时，他遇到了和他有着共同梦想的杜子华。杜子华研究生毕业后游历了美国、法国和加拿大，凭着对外语的透彻领悟和灵活运用，在国外结交了很多朋友，也得到了很多机会。但是他在国外待的时间越久、接触的人越多，就越是能感觉到提高民族素质的重要性和迫切性。

1994年，在北京做培训的杜子华接到了俞敏洪的电话。谈话中，俞敏洪向其讲述了新东方的创业和发展、自己的理想、对人才的渴望等。这次沟通改变了杜子华单打独斗实现教育梦的计划，杜子华决定在新东方实现自己的追求和梦想。1995年，俞敏洪来到加拿大邀请曾在北大共事的朋友徐小平回国加入新东方。随后，俞敏洪又来到美国邀请当时已经进入贝尔实验室工作的同学王强加入新东方。

1997年，俞敏洪的另一个同学包凡一也从加拿大赶回来，加入了新东方。新东方就像一个磁场，凝聚起一个个年轻人的梦想，年轻人身上积蓄的需要爆发的能量，在新东方得到了充分释放。1994—2000年，杜子华、徐小平、王强、胡敏、包凡一、何庆权、钱永强、江博、周成刚等人陆续被俞敏洪招揽到了新东方的旗下。

作为教育行业内的企业，师资构成了新东方的核心竞争力。俞敏洪从学生需求出发，秉持着"比别人做的多一点儿，比别人做的好一点儿"的创新思维，合理组建团队，寻找市场空白，使新东方的业务体系得以不断完善。比如，当时新东方提供出国咨询业务，学员可以获得包括基本申请步骤、各个国家对待留学生的区别、各个大学颁发奖学金的流程、读研和读博的区别等信息。

1995年，俞敏洪意识到学生对于英语培训的需求已经不只限于出国考试。1995年加入新东方的胡敏，开发出了广受欢迎的雅思英语考试培训。徐小平、王强、杜子华等人各尽其能，分别在出国咨询、基础英语、出版、网络等领域，为新东方搭起了一条顺畅的产品链，如徐小平开设的签证课、王强开设的"美语思维"训练法课，杜子华开设的"电影视听培训法"课等。

俞敏洪的成功之处是为新东方组建了一支年轻而又充满激情和智慧的团队。谈到团队的组建，《西游记》中的取经团队被公认是黄金组合，4个人的性格各不相同，却又各自有着不可替代的优势。比如说，唐僧以慈悲为怀，有使命感和组织设计能力，注重行为规范和工作标准，担任团队的主管，是团队的核心；孙悟空武功高强，能迅速理解、完成任务，是团队的业务骨干和铁腕人物；猪八戒虽然实力不高又好吃懒做，但是他善于活跃工作气氛，使取经之旅不至于太沉闷；沙僧勤恳踏实，平时默默无闻，关键时刻却能稳如泰山、稳定局面。

新东方的创业团队就有些类似于唐僧的取经团队。俞敏洪的温厚，王强的爽直，徐小平的激情，杜子华的洒脱，包凡一的稳重，5个人的鲜明个性让新东方总是处在一种不甘平庸的氛围当中。

俞敏洪敢于选择这些人做创业伙伴，并且成就了一个新东方的传奇，从这一点来说，他是一个成功的创业团队领导者。他清楚地了解新东方人都是性情中人，从来不掩饰自己的情绪，也不愿迎合他人的想法，打交道都是直来直去，有话直说。因此，在新东方形成了一种批判和宽容相结合的文化氛围。批判使新东方人敢于互相指责、纠正错误；宽容使新东方人在批判之后能够互相谅解、继续合作。

（资料来源：根据网络资料整理）

案例思考题：

1. 在创业路上，没有像《西游记》中那样的机会让你聚集黄金组合，如果只能从这4个人中选择2人来作为创业团队成员，你会挑选哪2个人？

2. 毫无疑问，俞敏洪是一位成功的创业团队领导者，你认为创业团队领导者应该具备哪些素质？

分析提示：

1. 创业者需要先知道自己拥有什么，才能知道他需要从别人那里得到什么。为了选择适应性更强的合作者，创业者必须首先从知识基础、专业技能、动机、承诺和个性特征等方面评估自己。

2. 创业团队的领导者一般应具有洞察力、有效的谈判技巧、团队管理和建设能力、乐观的态度、创新性、警觉性等素质。

案例 6

成江药业：创始人之间的裂痕如何修复？

知识点：

创业团队组建与评估、创业企业的特征、创业团队冲突与管理。

案例目的：

本案例通过孙家明与周云龙合作关系的变化，让学生了解创业团队的冲突和管理问题，从而探索创业团队关系的管理。

案例正文：

孙加明和周云龙是高中和大学的同学。大学毕业后，周云龙进入一家大型国有药厂从事质量检验工作，孙加明则被分配到一家国有化工厂从事技术研发工作。

在一次同学聚会上，两人有了一次深入交谈。他们都认为在现在就职的企业很难施展自己的才华。当时两人已经有了一定的积蓄，而且政策环境也比较好，可以共同创业。

1. 协力发展

1994年年初，两人从企业辞职。1994年2月，两人创办了一家合成化工厂，初始注册资金25万元，租用他人的场地和设备进行生产。周云龙负责产品销售和对外联络，孙加明负责技术、产品研发和生产。

由于孙加明肯钻研、技术研发能力强，周云龙人缘好、善于结交朋友，企业在第一年就试制舒胆通粗品并获得成功，取得销售收入50万元、利税10多万元的佳绩。1999年，企业增加注册资本到1500万元，并更名为成江医药化工有限责任公司，经营范围变更为医药中间体的制造及出口。2005年，企业增加注册资本到1亿元，当年营收近3亿元，净利润近8000万元。

在多年的合作中，两人一直是同比例增资，分工一直是孙加明对内、周云龙对外，相互间也一直保持坦诚和对彼此的信任。

2. 滋生裂痕

随着企业规模的不断扩大，企业的各种荣誉接踵而来。孙加明认为周云龙不应过于强调销售部门的重要性。为了规范企业内部管理，孙加明制订了很多的规章制度。他认为，违反了规章制度就应该照章处理。但周云龙却认为规章制度只是一种管理手段，特殊情况应该酌情处理。两人因此发生过几次争论。

自 2008 年国际金融危机以后，双方对企业的发展一直存在着不同的想法。孙加明认为，企业今后要坚持自己的特色，仍然以原料药为主、适度发展制剂，致力于进一步扩大在国内市场和在欧美市场的份额；要坚持技术导向，通过工艺改进和科技开发，持续提高产品收率、降低生产成本、提高产品质量，同时降低企业污染物的排放总量；要走专业化道路，集中精力做好医药产业。

周云龙则认为做企业，就应该处处领先别人一步，这样企业才有竞争力；应该学会借力，通过利用资本市场、兼并收购、多元化等实现企业的跨越式发展。周云龙提出，企业应该有开放的意识，善于借助资本市场的力量；做制剂、研发抗艾药都需要大量的投入，企业可以考虑引进风投、上市等，尽管这在一定程度上会稀释股份，但也可以增强企业实力、降低风险。他认为，虽然国际金融危机以来，市场形势不好，但这对于有志于进一步发展的企业来说，却是好时机。只要正确决策，通过产品结构的调整、科技含量的提高、资本力量的运用，今后几年企业保持 20%的净利润增长应该没问题。

3. 两难抉择

两人的分歧和矛盾不断增加。周云龙提出，由一人来全权负责企业经营，同时负责人必须达成今后三年保持 20% 的净利润增长率的目标，若失败，则要出让股份来补偿业绩差额，并让出经营管理权。周云龙同时承诺，可以由孙加明先选择。

孙加明认为，如果由自己负责，虽然获得了经营管理权，达成目标也会比较有成就感，但是要承担出让股份的风险。如果由周云龙负责，若他成功达成目标，则自己会失去经营管理权；若失败，虽然自己可以增加股份和获得经营管理权，但却存在事业毁于一旦的风险。因此，不管由谁来负责，风险都很大。

（资料来源：节选自邢以群．成江药业：创始人之间的合作裂痕如何修复？全国百篇优秀管理案例．中国管理案例共享中心，2012）

案例思考题：

1. 孙加明和周云龙为什么要一起创办企业而不是独自创业？

2. 成江制药为什么能在最初的十年中取得良好的业绩？其后孙加明和周云龙之间为什么会产生矛盾？

3. 如果你是孙加明，你会选择继续平等分工合作还是授权一人全权负责？如果选择继续分工合作，你应该如何做？

分析提示：

1. 创业大多采用团队合作的形式，良好的创业团队往往是创业成功的有效保证。创业者以团队形式进行创业，不仅可以获得资源上的补充，还能起到分散风险的作用。更重要的是，团队成员间的相互合作与鼓励，能起到减轻创业者心理负担、激励创业者成长的作用。

2. 创业初期，创业团队往往能通力协作。随着创业企业的成长，企业管理变得复杂起来，权利分配、利益分配等都会成为争夺的焦点。正所谓"共患难易，共富贵难"。

3. 多头领导往往会造成管理的混乱和权责不明，所以分工必须明确。创业团队的管理十分复杂，经常面临各种冲突，尤其是创始人之间的沟通、关系处理不当，都会造成各种矛盾。

案例 7

张朝阳的早期创业历程

知识点：

创业者与外部环境对机会识别的作用。

案例目的：

本案例适用于影响创业机会识别的因素分析，重点关注：①创业者在识别创业机会中的作用，可从警觉性、个人特质和认知学习能力等角度展开；②外部环境对创业机会识别的影响，如融资环境和市场环境对创业机会识别的影响。

案例正文：

张朝阳，1964年，出生于陕西西安市；1986年，毕业于清华大学物理系，同年取得李政道奖学金赴美留学，1993年，在美国麻省理工学院获得博士学位；1994年，任麻省理工学院亚太地区联络负责人；1995年，任美国爱思爱高科技有限公司（ISI）驻中国首席代表；1996年，创建了爱特信公司。1998年，爱特信正式推出搜狐产品，并更名为搜狐；2000年，搜狐在美国上市。

西安的地域文化，清华大学的校园文化和美国的西方现代文化，共同铸就了张朝阳的精神内核。他既沉默、务实，又新锐、前卫、时尚。

1995年7月，美国的硅谷式创业激起了张朝阳创业的热情，他认识到互联网经济具有惊人的商业和社会价值，于是决心回国创业。张朝阳联系ISI公司想做中国在线（China Online），ISI公司总裁的想法和张朝阳相近，两人一拍即合。1995年，张朝阳以ISI公司驻中国首席代表身份用互联网在中国收集和发布经济信息。

在ISI公司的经历，让张朝阳觉得中国互联网市场的潜力巨大。1998年2月，张朝阳推出第一家全中文的网上搜索引擎——搜狐。1998年3月，张朝阳获得英特尔等公司共210万美元的投资，他的事业开始蒸蒸日上。1998年9月，搜狐上海分公司成立，1999年6月，搜狐广州分公司开始组建。2000年，搜狐在美国成功上市,并收购了"中国人"社区网站。网络社区的规模性发展给门户网站加入了新的内涵,使搜狐成为中国最大的门户网站之一,为其业务迅速走上规模化奠定了基础。

随后,张朝阳判断出短信会给互联网带来巨大利益,并尝试把它作为一个能与互联网紧密结合的产业来运作。2001年,张朝阳耗资百万成就"搜狐手机时尚之旅",并担任首席形象代言人,带来了很好的效果。

2002年7月17日,搜狐实现盈利。2003年2月25日,搜狐推出游戏《骑士》,宣布进军网络游戏。在"2003年上市公司中国科技人物财富排行榜"上,张朝阳获得亚军;在胡润的"2003年中国IT富豪50强"中,张朝阳名列三甲。

1999—2001年,在中国的互联网市场进入高潮时,搜狐却在原地踏步,董事会也出现了问题。2001年3—4月,搜狐股票跌破1美元,有被纳斯达克摘牌的危险。当时的形势非常严峻,但张朝阳在这种困境下成功锤炼了自己。2001—2004年,张朝阳解决了问题,使搜狐最终脱离困境。

张朝阳认为搜狐走出困境并持续快速发展的原因,是自己和搜狐的管理层都具有较强的反思能力。正是这种反思能力,使张朝阳和搜狐的管理层认识到搜狐长于营销,短于产品的毛病。张朝阳认为,每个人都有自己特殊的成长经历,这必然导致认识上的偏颇,只有不断调整自己,对一切心存敬畏,才能突破自我,达到宠辱不惊。

(资料来源:郑炳章,2009.创业研究[M].北京:北京理工大学出版社)

案例思考题:

1. 基于本案例,分析创业者对创业机会识别的作用。
2. 分析外部环境对创业机会识别的作用。

分析提示:

1. 创业者的特征、经验、认知、社会网络关系、创造性等都会影响创业机会的识别。本问题可从张朝阳的警觉性、个人特质及认知学习能力等角度进行分析。

2.除了创业者自身因素外,外部环境同样对创业机会识别具有重要影响。机会识别过程是创业者和环境互动的结果,在这个过程中,创业者利用各种渠道和方式掌握并获取有关环境变化的信息,从而发现现实世界中在产品、服务、原材料和组织方式等方面存在的差距或缺陷,找到改进或创造"目的—手段"关系的可能性,最终识别出可能带来新产品、新服务、新原料和新组织方式的创业机会。本问题可从融资环境、市场环境等角度进行分析。

案例 8

E 公司的失败

知识点：

市场导向、团队组建、创业营销。

案例目的：

本案例的目的是让学生：①意识到创业过程中经常出现的一个严重问题——忽视客户，忽视市场；②了解新业务创建的复杂性以及合法性对初创企业的重要性。

案例正文：

2009年，王明发现储存和整理照片是一项困难的工作。他与工程师张强讨论时，发现对方也有关于处理照片的困惑。而且拍摄的照片越多，越不会回顾这些照片。

当时市场上还没有一个可以存储和整理照片，并在某种程度上鼓励人们经常回顾这些照片的产品。于是两人决定创业，建立一个提供照片存储和整理服务的模型。2011年6月，他们遇到了范华，并把他发展成了合伙人，后者曾经在上海的一家公司做交互和视觉设计工作。三人用几个月的时间设计了服务模型，并将其命名为EP。EP可以准确地在计算机桌面发现照片，并通过网络服务上传照片，而后整理照片并标记出最好的几张，方便、快捷并易于使用。

王明和张强将从天使投资人那里募集的180万美元投入产品开发。2013年3月，他们推出了EP第一个版本。通过连接到EP的App，用户可以看到过去的全部照片；如果支付一定的费用，就可以存储海量的照片。EP还有一个很棒的功能是闪回，它每天会给用户发一封电邮，内容是他们在历史上的今天所拍的照片。EP的服务好评如潮，用户们都很喜欢，App拥有1000多条用户评论，并获得了4.5星的评分。然而，2013年夏天，EP却突然停止运营了。

总体来看，EP的失败是因为其创始人花费了太多时间和精力来完善他们的服务。

EP 的订阅者并不能轻易地与朋友们分享照片，进而鼓励朋友们成为 EP 的用户，因为 EP 的服务并不是病毒式传播的。EP 的团队意识到了这个问题，并尝试用各种方法使服务的传播更快速，但都未成功。而且 EP 也没有在广告和营销上有任何投入，他们将资金全部投入到服务与产品的研发与完善中。因此，当其他的 App 吸引着大量的用户时，EP 的注册人数还不足 19000 人。

在破产的前几周，EP 的创始人仍试图募集更多的资金。但随着其他相关 App 数量的激增，用户可以轻易地在这些照片处理 App 中转换。而且当 EP 的商业模式还在依靠付费订阅的时候，许多 EP 的竞争对手的服务已经免费了。因此投资商们拒绝了他们。他们还向潜在收购者递交了一些提案，但最后也都失败了。最终，EP 因耗光了资金而只能停止运营了。

案例思考题：

1. 如果你打算创建企业来解决某个问题，请列出从案例中学习到的未来要规避的三个关键点。

2. 追求机会来解决问题与创建一家企业之间存在多大差异？在这方面 EP 犯了什么错误？

分析提示：

1. 创业需要以市场为导向，没有贴近市场、忽视顾客需要的创业必然会遭受失败。从创业团队的组建到公司的建立，再到创业营销、资源整合都是不可忽略的重要部分。忽略市场导向、忽略公司的建立、缺乏必要的创业营销策略、忽略后续商业模式的创新等都是导致 EP 失败的原因。

2. 追求机会来解决问题相对简单，但创建企业就变得复杂起来。企业的经营管理是多方面的、复杂的活动。而且，创建企业需要以机会为导向才更容易获得成功。

案例 9

实用的"修补术"

知识点：

资源拼凑、资源拼凑类型。

案例目的：

通过 2 个微案例，引导学生认识何为资源拼凑，资源拼凑的一般类型和优缺点。

案例正文：

毕克贵巧卖章鱼

2004 年，毕克贵接管了父母创办的企业。该企业主营鱼、贝和虾等产品的出口加工，年销售额 2000 多万元。随着原料及生产成本不断上涨，公司利润越来越低。于是毕克贵打出招商广告，以寻找更多机会。

2006 年，某日本企业代表于洋找到毕克贵，希望以每吨成品章鱼 6000 美元的价格，签一份价值 50 万美元的订单。这是因为毕克贵有一条位于单独车间的闲置生产线，符合日方生产要求。大连本地的章鱼不是客户需要的品种，为了寻找原料，毕克贵去福建收购了 150 吨章鱼，按照客户的要求进行加工。这单生意使毕克贵赚了 4 万多美元。更重要的是，以后每月都有 20 万美元的订单。在其他海产品加工还照常生产的情况下，企业产值翻了一番。

出口到日本的是章鱼头和章鱼爪，剩下的脖子和爪尖由于是规格外产品，只能积压在仓库里。2007 年 4 月，毕克贵在逛街时发现有人在卖用鱿鱼爪子做的章鱼丸子。销售商称，章鱼原料难找，只好用鱿鱼替代。于是毕克贵将规格外产品卖给销售商，每年工厂又增加了 20 万元利润。同时，毕克贵了解到章鱼丸子一盒卖 3 元钱，而成本不到 3 角，这给他很大触动。在传统理念中，出口加工企业一般只专注于控制成本，很少去考虑市场和销售的问题。毕克贵希望摆脱单纯靠加工产品、挣加工费的经营方式，能够直接销售自己的产品。

2008年春节,针对市民春节采购的需要,毕克贵把鱼虾类产品做成礼盒销售。毕克贵推销礼盒时,认识了大连的海参经销商王振东。经过协商,毕克贵以40%的销售利润作回报,将海鲜休闲产品放到王振东的海参专卖店里销售。王振东卖海参、鲍鱼,毕克贵销售海鲜休闲食品,二者互补,不到一个月海鲜休闲食品的销售额就突破10万元。

迅雷的早期创业历程

2002年,迅雷创始人程浩和邹胜龙共同创业,但没过多久公司就陷入了困境,于是两人商量转型。程浩发现,在互联网5大应用——门户、邮箱、搜索、即时通信、下载中,唯独下载没有主流提供商。但对于大容量文件(如电影、网络游戏),用户必须通过下载才能使用。于是程浩和邹胜龙决定研发迅雷。迅雷采用基于网格原理的多资源超线程技术,下载速度非常快。为了能用最快的速度发布产品,程浩在研发过程中放弃了对产品其他细节的研究,只关注目标消费者最关心的特性问题。早期版本虽然存在很多漏洞,但凭借速度优势,迅雷在市场上抢占了先机。

2004年,程浩找到金山软件的总裁雷军,雷军给了他一次测试的机会。测试显示,迅雷的下载速度是其他工具的20倍。于是金山软件同意推荐其游戏用户使用迅雷免费下载其热门游戏的客户端软件。在获得金山软件的认同后,迅雷很快和其他网络游戏厂商达成协议。两个月后,迅雷每天的新增用户量就由不到300增加到1万多。半年时间,迅雷拥有了300万用户,95%的用户是由网游合作伙伴带来的。有了可观的用户群后,迅雷很快通过广告、软件捆绑、无线、按效果付费的竞价排名广告等渠道获得了收支平衡。随后,迅雷不断推出升级版本修正软件漏洞。

(资料来源:1.田新,王晓文.案例讨论 如何实施拼凑策略[J].企业管理,2009,No.333(05):9-11;

2.王晓文,田新.拼凑双刃剑:迷失还是超越[J].企业管理,2009,No.333(05):6-8)

案例思考题：

1. 何为资源拼凑？毕克贵是如何实施资源拼凑的？
2. 迅雷采取了何种资源拼凑，为什么？

分析提示：

1. 资源拼凑包含三个关键要素：利用手边的已有资源、整合资源用于新目的和将就使用。毕业贵在创业过程中，不断利用手边的各种资源寻找新机会，如突破习惯的思维方式、对手边资源进行再利用、将就使用、整合资源等。

2. 资源拼凑一般可以分为全面拼凑和选择性拼凑。全面拼凑是指创业者在物质资源、人力资源、技术资源、制度规范和顾客市场等方面长期使用拼凑方法，在企业现金流步入稳定后依然没有停止拼凑行为。这种行为导致企业在内部经营管理上难以形成符合标准的规章制度，在外部市场上也会因为采用低标准资源遇到阻力，使企业无法走上正轨。选择性拼凑是指创业者在拼凑行为上有一定的选择性。在应用领域上，他们往往只选择在一两个领域内进行拼凑，以避免全面拼凑的那种自我循坏；在应用时间上，他们只在早期创业资源紧缺的情况下采用拼凑。迅雷在早期产品研发上进行了选择性拼凑，在产品获得市场的认可后，放弃了选择性拼凑，而是转变为不断对产品进行优化（资源优化）。

案例 10

朗明科技的 AI 创业之路

知识点：

Timmons 创业要素模型、创业机会、创业资源、企业家精神。

案例目的：

通过本案例，使学生深入了解 Timmons 创业要素模型在创业中的运用；了解在不同创业阶段，创业者对机会的识别及对资源的把握；学习案例中郭明作为一名创业者在朗明科技不同阶段的发展过程中所展现的企业家精神。

案例正文：

1. 创业启蒙期

2009 年 7 月，21 岁的郭明从清华大学计算机科学实验班毕业，此实验班也就是"姚班"，由姚期智院士创办。毕业时郭明已在北京微软亚洲研究院实习了 2 年，当时他正参与计算机视觉人脸识别项目的研发。在这期间郭明接触和参与了很多行业前沿项目，直觉告诉他，计算机视觉技术未来大有可为。

毕业时，郭明将他的直觉和想法告诉了同在微软实习过的同学唐侠，两人遂决定以后一起创业。郭明认为，硬件和软件是人工智能的双翼，而他们只有软件技术，对相关的硬件知识知之甚少，所以他计划先去美国斯坦福大学学习 3D 相机方面的硬件知识，待学有所成后再回国创业。此时国内热门的是电商、团购、游戏，人工智能还未进入大众的视野。唐侠当时在中国信息学奥林匹克集训队任教练，他向郭明推荐了"姚班"的学弟张斌，这样三人创业团队的雏形就形成了。

2010 年，三人参加了全国"挑战杯"大赛，做了一款基于人脸识别和人脸追踪技术的游戏——《乌鸦来了》，最终获得冠军。这款游戏吸引了联想之星的关注。联想之星非常看好这款技术的市场价值，决定给予天使投资，希望三人能继续推出其他产品并进行市场化，同时邀请他们参加联想之星的 CEO 特训班，学习创业管理实践知识。

自接触到联想之星后，郭明就有了成立公司的想法。2011 年，朗明科技有限公司（以下简称朗明科技）在北京成立，郭明任 CEO。但郭明出国学习的计划并未改变，因为他始终认为人工智能技术一定要软硬件结合。公司成立不久，郭明便去了美国留学，唐侠和张斌则去联想之星 CEO 特训班学习，朗明科技暂以游戏开发维持运营，公司事务由三人通过视频会议沟通决定。三人的创业事迹在"姚班"引起了轰动，数十位"姚班"师弟来到刚成立不久的朗明科技实习。

2. 创业初创期

郭明内心并不认为游戏是他们的发展方向，毕竟他们不热衷游戏。一天，郭明看到了这样一则新闻："脸书（Facebook）以高达 1 亿美元的价格，收购了以色列一家成立不足一年的人脸识别公司"，这给郭明带来很大的震撼，随即他把这则消息告诉了唐侠和张斌，并提议暂停游戏的开发，集中全力将人脸识别技术研发出来，但其余二人却不以为然。

为了说服二人，郭明查阅了大量资料并请教了姚期智教授，同时，他还从美国的老师和同学那里了解到不仅是 Facebook，谷歌也斥资下注人脸识别，最终他得出结论：人工智能领域中，图像识别技术是具有代表性的应用场景，而人脸识别可能是衡量这个技术最好的一种方式。基于这些，朗明科技发展战略逐步清晰：围绕计算机视觉技术发展，公司的第一步是技术识人，第二步是识别万物，第三步是希望实现所见即所得的"机器之眼"。在这些资料和公司清晰的战略下，唐侠和张斌最终同意了郭明的提议。

2012 年 8 月，朗明科技完成了由联想之星和联想创投参与的天使投资，之后全力投入人脸识别技术的研发当中。同年 10 月，朗明科技正式发布了云端计算机视觉开放平台 Face++，在当时人工智能还没有普及的环境下，Face++ 平台就可以提供一整套世界领先的人脸检测、人脸识别、面部分析的视觉技术服务。Face++ 平台开放后不久，便开始和美图秀秀、世纪佳缘等客户合作。

虽然人脸识别技术有了阶段性的成果，但郭明深知作为一家技术服务公司，技术是最核心的竞争力，于是他提出了在公司成立技术研究院，专门进行技术持续迭代研发的想法。这一想法引来了其余两人的反对，他们认为Face++平台刚发布不久，缺少清晰的商业模式，不应该分散精力去毫无节制地搞技术研发。2013年5月，郭明辍学回国，筹备成立朗明研究院。他本想邀请在微软实习时的老师孙杨加入，但被婉拒。孙杨告诉郭明创新工场CEO李开复有意投资Face++平台。这样，2013年7月，朗明科技完成了由创新工场参与的A轮融资。

朗明科技把重点放到了内部人才的培养上，这时唐侠在中国信息学奥林匹克集训队任教练的经历便发挥了巨大的作用。朗明研究院最早的一批研究员和工程师，都是在信息学奥林匹克竞赛中拿过奖牌的选手。而且朗明科技打造了一个"技术信仰"的环境，吸引了很多清华、北大和北航的学生来实习，很多学生在实习期结束后就自然地留了下来。

2013年10月，人工智能算法引擎Brain++在朗明研究院投入研发。基于Brain++，朗明科技构建了一条不断自我改进、不断更加自动化的算法生产线，同时，Brain++也能针对不同垂直领域的碎片化需求，定制丰富且不断增长的算法组合。

3. 创业发展期

2014年，朗明科技与蚂蚁金服开始合作。2015年3月16日，在德国汉诺威IT博览会上，马云现场演示了蚂蚁金服的扫脸支付技术，其背后的技术就是朗明科技的人脸识别技术。同年，朗明科技完成了由创新工场及启明创投参与的B轮融资。

自人脸识别技术助力蚂蚁金服后，朗明科技便在B端市场上站稳了脚跟，这更让郭明意识到了人工智能技术赋能传统产业的巨大意义。于是郭明跟另外两位联合创始人决定将业务转向B端市场，果断放弃了已开发成功的火爆游戏及App等C端产品。

面对B端市场，朗明科技首先选择从已有经验积累的金融领域开辟市场，并推出了一款金融级身份验证解决方案FaceID，针对远程实名场景提供在线身份验证服务，被平安银行、中信银行、江苏银行等金融机构所采用。2015年10月，朗明科技发布了世界上第一台智能摄像机，该智能摄像机成为日后安防领域的硬件承载。自 2015 年 12 月为乌镇举办的"世界互联网大会"提供安保技术支持后，朗明科技便开始提供城市管理解决方案。此后，朗明科技陆续参与了 2016 年 G20 杭州峰会、2017 年厦门金砖峰会的安保工作。此外，朗明科技和公安部门合作，搭建了"三逃"人员的身份证图片库，依靠在公共场所的监控摄像头进行实时比对。

在企业不断发展壮大的同时，朗明科技组织管理开始出现问题，为此，郭明到湖畔大学学习组织管理和商业管理。

经过在金融和安防两大领域的拓展，2016 年，朗明科技成为中国计算机视觉领域的头部企业。这时郭明在微软实习时的老师孙杨加盟朗明科技，担任朗明研究院院长以及朗明科技的首席科学家。此后，朗明美国研究院、朗明南京研究院、朗明上海研究院等依次成立，这些研究院的重要负责人都是孙杨聘请的，其中朗明美国研究院的负责人由孙杨邀请前 Adobe 首席科学家李琳担任。

郭明认为，产学研结合是检验当下人工智能创新是否有价值的一个工具，所以朗明科技需要成立一个学术委员会。为此，郭明邀请姚期智教授担任学术委员会首席顾问。

唐侠一个偶然的机会发现，在南京天猫超市的一个 2 万平米的仓库，拣货员们每天要来回走约 40 公里进行作业。唐侠便开始琢磨用智能手段提高仓储物流作业的效率的可能性。2018 年 4 月，朗明科技收购了一家机器人公司，然后专注深度学习的机器视觉和智能调度算法技术研究。2019 年 1 月，朗明科技的技术团队领先业界研制并发布了物流制造领域首款人工智能物联网操作系统。朗明科技自主研发的人工智能技术可将机器人和仓储业务进行数字化链接，实现智能搬运、拣选等，该技术已被天猫超市、宝洁等采用。

案例思考题：

1. 影响创业成功的因素有哪些？你认为朗明科技创业启蒙期、初创期喜忧参半，但创业发展期业务开展顺利的原因有哪些？

2. 郭明在创业的三个阶段中，识别了哪些创业机会？他是如何做到准确识别的？

3. 郭明在创业过程中，分别运用了哪些有利资源？

4. 你认为郭明身上展现出的哪些特质与他的成功息息相关？郭明在创业过程中体现的企业家精神有哪些？

分析提示：

1. Timmons创业要素模型认为，成功的创业活动必须对机会、团队和资源三者进行恰当匹配，并要随着创业活动的发展而不断进行动态平衡。创业过程由机会启动，在创业前期，机会发掘与选择最为关键；创业初期的重点则在于组建创业团队，新事业启动后，才会产生增加资源的需求。所以，我们可以从Timmons创业要素模型进行分析。在创业启蒙期，朗明科技机会较多但定位模糊，人力、技术专家等资源相对丰富，团队检验不足，模型重心向右偏移，最终导致创业启蒙期发展比较缓慢。在创业初创期，此时创业机会与方向已明确，外界各种资源多但难获取，模型重心向左偏移，同样也处于一种不平衡的状态。在创业发展期，朗明科技在机会、团队与资源上实现了相对平衡，从而使得公司的新业务得到顺利开展。

2. 先前经验、认知因素、社会网络关系及创业警觉性是影响机会识别的关键因素。在创业启蒙期，郭明在北京微软的实习经历使他认识到计算机视觉技术的重要性，为此他告诉了同学唐侠，两人遂决定创业。在创业初创期，脸书以高达1亿美元的价格，收购了以色列一家成立不足一年的人脸识别公司，这使郭明认识到人脸识别技术的发展趋势。为此，他收集资料，朗明科技的发展战略与方向得以清晰。在创业发展期，朗明及时放弃C端市场，发力B端市场，这是郭明对创业机会的再次成功识别。

3. 创业资源是指新创企业在创造价值的过程中需要的特定资产，按照资产的形态可分为有形和无形资源。它是新创企业创立和运营的必要条件。在创业启蒙期，资源体现在：微软实习的机会、"挑战杯"的机会、联想之星的投资、"姚班"学弟们的支持等；在创业初创期，资源体现在：李开复的支持、清华、北大及北航学生的加入等；在创业发展期，资源体现在：与蚂蚁金服的合作、不断的融资、孙杨及李琳等人才的加入等。

4.创业者特质通常有四个维度：成就需求、内控制源、风险偏好及创新能力。企业家精神指企业家组织建立和经营管理企业的综合才能的表述方式，它是一种重要而特殊的无形生产要素，是企业家所具有的独特的个人素质、价值取向以及思维模式的抽象表达。具体来说，企业家精神包括创新精神、冒险精神、创业精神和宽容精神。

案例 11

叮咚买菜的商业模式

知识点：

PEST 分析、商业模式要素。

案例目的：

通过案例学习，学生将熟悉企业应如何根据市场环境设计商业模式，了解新零售环境下影响商业模式内容设计的因素，掌握商业模式画布设计的一般逻辑过程。

案例正文：

1. 乘势而起

2017 年 5 月，退役军人梁昌霖创立了叮咚买菜，致力于解决用户买菜难的问题。在四年时间里，叮咚买菜从上海起步，发展到长三角大部分地区，并进一步发展至北京、广州、深圳、成都、东莞、佛山等，致力于通过产地直采、前置仓配货和最快 29 分钟配送到家的服务模式，结合技术驱动产业链升级，为用户提供品质确定、时间确定、品类确定的生鲜消费体验，成为用户信赖的民生互联网企业。

在生鲜电商市场，有"盒马生鲜""每日优鲜"等，运营模式百花齐放，如盒马生鲜的"独立门店＋自提"的社区电商模式，美团优选、多多买菜的以"团长制＋自提"为主的社区团购模式等。在起初的"创业艰难百战多"的征途中，叮咚买菜愈挫愈勇。经过调研、选址、进设备、定品类，叮咚买菜终于找到了避免同质化竞争，实现差异化发展的成功之路——前置仓模式。

作为互联网经济较早的受益者，物流行业自然也进入了飞速发展的新时期。2016 年，国家发改委编制的《营造良好市场环境推动交通物流融合发展实施方案》提出，到 2020 年形成一批有较强竞争力的交通物流企业，完善冷链运输服务规范，实现全程不断链。从产地到餐桌，商品配送时间越来越短，我国冷链物流的快速发展给生鲜电商行业的发展带来了更多的可能性。

近年来,国家出台多项政策鼓励农业电商发展,生鲜市场面临巨大机遇。2019年,《关于推动农商互联完善农产品供应链的通知》(财办建〔2019〕69号)提出,加强农产品产后商品化处理设施、冷链物流设施,中央财政资金支持农产品产后商品化处理设施和冷链物流两类项目的资金比例不得低于70%。

互联网时代,人们消费观念的不断转变促使生鲜电商行业不断发展,给叮咚买菜带来了市场机遇。同时,许多不利于外卖行业的现象也随之而来,如"养生潮"的兴起使一些注重养生的人开始自己做菜。此外,生鲜行业在行业规模与技术环境方面迎来了转型期,一是农村土地流转,农业企业化;二是叮咚买菜等新零售企业规模不断扩大,倒逼上游企业提高品质和服务;三是中国的物流、大数据、人工智能等技术都在快速发展,行业价值链的中间环节被迅速优化。

2. 成功秘籍

(1)强基础

叮咚买菜在市场中的份额日益增加,这与其本身所具有的强大的实力和基础密不可分。稳定的生鲜农产品供应商、前置仓配货29分钟送达、强大的大数据分析能力、不断扩大的市场规模、大量资本投资、高复购率和服务水平等促进了叮咚买菜的长足发展。

稳定的生鲜农产品供应商。叮咚买菜的采购模式主要为"城批采购+品牌商直供"。对于蔬菜、水产等难以长途运输的生鲜产品,叮咚买菜采用"城批采购"为主的模式,以保障产品的鲜度并降低损耗。在这种模式下,补货更为容易、产品比较齐全、价格也相对稳定。而肉类产品则由品牌商按需直供,以保障产品的安全性及品质。

前置仓配货29分钟送达。叮咚买菜采取分布式仓储,而不是集中式仓储,这就为叮咚买菜的高配送效率奠定了基础。"29分钟+0配送费+0起送"更好地满足了即时消费需求。此外,在配送方面,叮咚买菜有多年的服务经验、稳定性较强的配送团队及一套自己研发的智能调度和末端配送系统,这为其高效率的配送服务奠定了基础。

强大的大数据分析能力。叮咚买菜将大数据贯穿于整个产业链,通过订单预测、用户画像、智能推荐、智能调度、路径优化、自助客服等技术，提升用户体验。据数据显示，叮咚买菜的大数据分析使其平均每日滞销损耗率低于3%，物流损耗率仅为0.3%。

不断扩大的市场规模。叮咚买菜在长三角市场进行了较为深入的布局。2019年春节期间，叮咚买菜宣布进入杭州，随后又陆续进入苏州、宁波、无锡等城市。虽然叮咚买菜进入了长三角多个城市，但还是以上海为中心，在上海周围200千米的范围内进行密集的布点。这也意味着，从供应链的角度来看，不同城市的叮咚买菜在供应链上的共享上成为可能。2019年8月，叮咚买菜正式进入深圳。进入深圳前，叮咚买菜团队仅用46天就完成了前期用户调研、供应链后台搭建、总仓和前置仓开设、一线人员配置等准备工作。

大量资本投资。作为生鲜电商中的一匹黑马，叮咚买菜广受资本青睐。叮咚买菜已经完成了多轮融资，投资方包括今日资本、红杉资本等一线投资机构。仅2018年，叮咚买菜就连续完成了5轮融资。

高复购率和服务水平。叮咚买菜尤其看重用户的长期留存，并提出"复购率为王"的策略。数据显示，叮咚买菜第31个月长期留存率为38%，老用户月均消费6.5次，处于行业领先水平。叮咚买菜App内设的"菜谱推荐"也增加了一定的黏着度，用户点击一个商品，商品详情的下方都会显示菜谱，同时给出对应食材和调料的购买链接，方便用户"一站式"购齐食材。

专注"卖菜"，客单价较低。叮咚买菜的产品结构中生鲜占比高达75%～80%，进入新城市时以"0元起送、0元配送费"降低用户购买门槛，因此客单价较低。数据显示，2017年，叮咚买菜客单价是30～40元；2018年，客单价达到了50元左右；2019年，叮咚买菜在上海部分区域做了客单28元以下收5元配送费的测试，客单价上升至60元。

（2）寻外力

叮咚买菜业务的顺利开展离不开供应链上的每个环节，叮咚买菜通过与各位合作伙伴进行协同合作，竭力追求双赢共进。

叮咚买菜与上海农场签署了战略合作协议,并将上海农场授牌为"叮咚买菜合作基地",共同推进上海农产品产销一体化转型升级,推广线上线下一体化的生鲜新零售模式。与此同时,叮咚买菜与200多家合作社、3000多个农户进行合作,实现源头直采。源头直采减少了中间商等环节,最大限度减少损耗,保持产品的新鲜度,并且降低了成本。

2019年,在阿里本地生活生鲜伙伴大会上,叮咚买菜与口碑"饿了么"签署战略合作协议,未来将共同探索包括物流、营销、售后、会员等在内的各类合作方向。叮咚买菜成为阿里本地生活生态合作伙伴中的重要一员。

叮咚买菜一直采用前置仓模式来实现"到家"的买菜服务,为缩短最后一千米,叮咚买菜在城市的各个社区集中点位设置前置仓,保证一种密度高的小型仓储模式。因此,仓储出租方成为叮咚买菜极为重要的合作伙伴。如何通过与出租方达成友好合作来获得优质仓储位置,一直是叮咚买菜的关注重点。

(3)明确的目标客户

叮咚买菜的目标客户可以分为以下4类。

餐饮企业。叮咚买菜与餐饮企业在人力、食材、供应链方面达成战略合作,为餐饮企业输送优质生鲜。

生活节奏快的上班族。当今时代人们的生活节奏加快,上班族往往很难有时间为自己做一顿饭。去一个可靠的菜市场、选菜、回家处理,这些需要花费大量的时间。上班族工作日过于忙碌,周末时宅在家中,叮咚买菜送菜上门服务可谓是为其量身定做的。

腿脚不便的老年人。许多老年人年纪大了腿脚不方便,如果附近的菜市场离家比较远就不方便去买菜。叮咚买菜送菜上门服务既满足了老年人自己做菜的心愿,又避免了出行给他们身体带来的负担。

租赁企业。叮咚买菜将闲置的冷库暂时出租给其他企业或个人。

(4)多样营销模式与多种收入来源

叮咚买菜的营销模式有以下几种:①老带新奖励制;②绿卡会员制;③大数据

预测与智能推荐。叮咚买菜的主要收入，包括为用户提供新鲜蔬菜、水果、海鲜等生鲜产品的销售收入；平台服务佣金；App 广告收入；绿卡每年每人 88 元的会员费；冷库租赁收入；仓储物流平台配套服务收入。叮咚买菜的成本结构主要包括生鲜采购、储存和冷链配送费用；人力成本；前置仓修建、购买和租用费用；轻营销推广费用、App 开发和大数据算法成本，以及网站运营维护成本。

（资料来源：1.沈羽.叮咚买菜：生鲜新零售赛道黑马突围记［J］.上海企业，2021，（08）：24-29；

2.马龙波，王晓颖.叮咚买菜何以成"黑马"［J］.企业管理，2021，（08）：78-81）

案例思考题：

1.目前叮咚买菜所处的环境如何？试运用 PEST 进行分析。

2.基于商业模式画布，分析叮咚买菜的商业模式。

3.叮咚买菜是如何确定并吸引目标用户的？这些用户具有怎么样的特点？

分析提示：

1.PEST 分析是指对企业生存与发展的宏观环境的分析，P 是政治、E 是经济、S 是社会、T 是技术。经济方面，主要内容有经济发展水平、规模、增长率、政府收支、通货膨胀率等；政治方面，主要内容有政治制度、政府政策、国家的产业政策、相关法律和法规等；社会方面，主要内容有人口、价值观念、道德水平等；技术方面，主要内容有高新技术、工艺技术和基础研究的突破性进展等。

2.商业模式是企业创造价值的核心逻辑。商业模式的这一逻辑性主要表现在以下方面：①价值发现，明确价值创造的来源，企业最终的盈利与否取决于它是否拥有顾客；②价值匹配，明确合作伙伴，实现价值创造；③价值获取，制定竞争策略，占有创新价值。商业模式包含以下关键要素：客户细分、价值主张、渠道通路、客户关系、收入来源、核心资源、关键业务、重要伙伴、成本结构。

3. 目标用户群体是公司所瞄准的用户群体。这些群体具有某些共性，从而使公司能够创造价值。本题分为三个部分：确定用户、吸引用户、用户特点。叮咚买菜从自身服务内容、目标用户特点及大数据分析等来确定用户；通过菜谱推荐、拼团、地摊及微信等手段吸引用户；用户特点则可以在五类用户描述中进行总结。

案例 12

悦管家的商业模式创新之路

知识点：

商业模式画布、商业模式创新、商业模式价值创造逻辑。

案例目的：

通过本案例的学习，学生将了解商业模式的价值创造逻辑，掌握商业模式画布分析工具，进而具备运用商业模式画布的价值创造逻辑对商业模式进行分析的能力。

案例正文：

1. 模式 1.0

2012 年 12 月 12 日，悦管家注册成立，管理团队只有李尉一人是全职。刘珺是创始股东之一，但他并未正式加入管理团队。虽然悦管家的定位是互联网家政公司，但其发展策略是"线下 2C，从人开始"："线下 2C"是指因资源约束，从线下逐步向 O2O 过渡；"从人开始"是指要想提升服务，需要先提升服务人员的服务能力和职业热情。

2013 年，悦管家的家政服务培训教室落地，教室面积仅 100 平方米，最多能同时容纳 80~100 人。2013—2014 年，李尉对 4000 多名服务人员进行了专业技能培训，培训内容包括服务标准、服务技能、服务形象及礼仪、沟通技巧等。

有很多人问李尉，每年的培训可以输出 2000 名服务人员，但只有 20% 的人会选择加入悦管家，值得吗？李尉觉得值得的原因有以下四点。第一，家政服务人员普遍缺乏专业性，家政培训很必要。第二，家政服务人员一般被认为只能输出低效、重复且低价值的劳动，收入水平普遍偏低。但服务人员通过精进家政服务相关的技能，能降本增效，创造更多收入。第三，家政业没有统一的标准，服务质量和效果全靠服务人员自己把握。既然没有现成的标准，那由企业建立和实践标准最为可行。第四，服务人员年龄普遍偏高，多数集中在 40~50 岁，然而，服务人员年轻化是趋势，通过培训，提高服务人员的相关业务知识水平和竞争力，将家政服务行业从低门槛、低水平转变为有门槛、高水平的行业，从而吸引更多年轻人加入。

进行培训的同时，悦管家的第一家线下服务支持和补给站（以下简称门店，也就是后来的云店）也开张了。门店装修简单，区域主要划分为服务咨询台、物品置放区、休息区、电瓶充电区及卫生间。服务咨询台主要由店长负责，用来接单、派单、收银等。物品置放区，被用来规整地存放服务用具及物料。休息区、电瓶充电区及卫生间则是针对服务人员设计的补给站，服务人员可以在休息区免费接热水喝、热饭、吹空调、聊天和休息，休息间隙还可以给电瓶充电。

说到卫生间，这是门店的特色，市场上同类的服务门店是不会自建卫生间的。当门店配备了卫生间后，3千米服务半径内的服务人员都可以使用。门店的第一要务是为服务人员提供基础条件，如有时还会选择租用小区内的公寓而非店铺，因为这样还能顺带解决店长的住宿问题。

门店的经营看似简单，但并非每一位店长在一开始就能理解建设门店的初衷。曾有店长为了节省成本，限制夏季纯净水的供应量，导致出现服务人员没水喝的情况。李尉得知后，立即与该店长沟通，夏天温度高，饮水量大，每天每个门店平均要消耗三桶水。门店作为服务人员的后勤管理和补给站，如果最基本的饮用水都要限制，势必影响服务人员的工作积极性和服务质量。

2012—2014年，李尉将工作重心放在了培训和建设门店上，集中精力主攻服务供应链的上游，通过微博、微信和广告对目标客户进行推广，但这一期间悦管家的营业收入增长缓慢。

2. 模式2.0

2014年，悦管家账户资金见底，创始人开始讨论外部融资的问题。2015年，悦管家获得了金巍管理500万元的风险投资。这是悦管家成立以来的第一笔外部融资。

外部融资成功后，悦管家选择投身O2O大军，将线下开店的模式转变为线上引流、线下服务输出的O2O家政服务模式。2015年，"悦管家Life" App上线，悦管家正式开启家政服务的互联网探索之路。

悦管家 O2O 服务云平台连接上游服务人员和下游用户。一方面，百度、58 同城等引流来的用户可以通过平台浏览服务种类、服务包含的具体内容和价格等。另一方面，服务人员可以通过悦管家 O2O 服务云平台优化服务品质。

在初期专注线下开店时，李尉就意识到改变和培养家政服务人员和管理者才是这个行业发展的核心，所以悦管家团队在人力资源建设上的探索从未止步。

悦管家的人力资源建设主要分为针对管理运营团队的核心岗位人员培养与激励，以及针对服务实施的基层岗位人员的培养两部分。对前者，悦管家主要通过期权和有限合伙股权方式给予激励。而对人员数量相对较大的后者，悦管家采用了关键岗位遴选与使用机制。服务人员通过考核后即可提高自己的服务星级，星级服务人员积累服务经验到一定阶段后可以成为悦管家线下门店的合伙人，完成从服务人员向管理者的角色转换与升级。

悦管家进入 O2O 领域时，该领域已经过了市场最疯狂的时期，但补贴似乎成了互联网产品推广的标配。当悦管家在服务人员培训和考核的基础建设阶段努力时，竞争对手通过补贴已获得了大量用户。互联网求快速发展，投资人也偏好能快速增长的项目，如果悦管家只是在人力资源建设上精耕细作，而无法提高订单量，那么培训出来的服务人员也会去其他有更多订单的平台，剩下的市场份额也会也越来越少。

经过讨论，悦管家决定开始实行战略补贴，基础保洁服务每小时的服务单价降低了 10 元。但对悦管家来说，每小时服务从产生 3.5 元的盈利变成了 6.5 元的亏损。这一轮补贴对悦管家获客产生了明显的效果，家庭基础清洁服务的月销售量突破了 1 万单。

3. 模式 3.0

在这个重要节点上，悦管家的管理决策团队迎来了一位新成员——刘珺，她也是悦管家的创始股东之一。刘珺出任 CEO 后，不仅让公司内部的经营管理逐渐步入正轨，还为深陷 O2O 补贴大战的悦管家找到了一条出路。

刘珺认为，在大平台合并、外部资本停止持续注入、补贴逐渐消失的时候，悦管家的现金流及成本—收益的管控越发显得重要。现金流是企业生存和扩张的基本条件。悦管家当下发展模式的缺陷主要为：第一，补贴推广效果不如预期；第二，C端服务的时间高度集中，资源配置效率待优化；第三，服务品类较为单一，服务体系待完善，无法形成比较优势。

因此，刘珺在成为悦管家CEO之后做的第一个决定就是砍掉不赚钱的业务，停止补贴获客。这个改变导致订单量从每月1万多单跌至2000多单，平台的服务人员也因收入减少而大量流失。为了稳住服务人员，悦管家调整服务人员的劳务收入，支付远距离补贴，并组织专人与服务人员谈心。在取消补贴后的第四个月，C端保洁服务的月订单恢复到调整前的水平。

当发现工作日和休息日家庭服务需求量失衡的情况时，悦管家决定开拓发展B端业务，该业务主要包括民宿保洁、酒店保洁、公寓保洁，以及办公物业保洁。因为B端业务的服务时间正好与C端业务的高峰期互补，所以悦管家的服务人员多数情况下能被分配到更合适的订单。

爱彼迎是全球民宿巨头，它在进入中国后碰到了保洁难题。因此，爱彼迎开始寻找中国的保洁供应商，并最终选择了悦管家。在爱彼迎平台上，房东可在线预约悦管家的清洁服务，悦管家的系统会即时得到订单，并自动确认服务时间和分配服务人员。对爱彼迎来说，通过这种与第三方合作的方式，不仅保洁成本降低30%以上，而且还能为住客提供更好的体验。

悦管家在不断优化保洁服务效率的过程中，也逐渐触碰到了行业当前所能达到的天花板，渐渐地，所投入的成本与产出的效益不再平衡了。如何在维持自身保洁服务质量的同时，开发新品类单品，一直困扰着刘珺及其团队。

2017年1月，刘珺机缘巧合下接触到了膳食领域的合作方。刘珺突然发现膳食餐饮有着巨大市场需求，而且可复制性非常高。于是，悦管家在漕河泾开发区开了第一家园区餐厅，依托无油烟的中央厨房，为开发区的上班族提供健康的餐食。但由于用户对食物不满意，第一家悦管家餐厅很快就失败了。

这一次失败没有打倒刘珺及其团队，悦管家通过从德国采购先进的微厨设备，提升了饭菜的口感；并通过中央工厂的预处理和标准操作流程供应食材，使厨师在现场只需要掌握火候和精加工即可。为了提升用户体验,悦管家还在园区食堂引入了人脸识别。

在悦管家的客户中,首届进口博览会、国家奥林匹克体育中心、中国政法大学、中国地质大学、中国计量院、漕河泾园区、上实、百联等赫然在列。而企业服务也成为悦管家向新城市复制扩张的切入点。

在思考如何有效管控上游服务人员的时候,刘珺及其团队参考稻盛和夫提出的"阿米巴"模式开发了"云店"合伙人发展模式。"云店"是在公司内部管理以外设立的针对服务人员招募、培训、管理的单元,其前身是早期的线下门店。"云店"合伙人负责日常管理和运营,一般是从具有较高年资、较好业绩、经验丰富的服务人员中选出。通过努力,悦管家4年间营业收入增长了150多倍,"2C+2B,时间共享"的模式也得到了投资人的认可。2017年,悦管家以超过2亿元的估值拿到了数千万元的投资。

4. 模式 4.0

家政服务行业的竞争程度显然超出了刘珺的想象。刘珺从战略角度对消费者、服务者、经营者进行分析,发现:在消费者端,年轻人逐步成为消费主力军,他们的家政需求出现了明显的升级;在服务者端,一方面合格家政服务人员的有效供给严重不足,另一方面服务人员的职场获得感不强,人员流动性大;在经营者端,家政企业由于提供的是上门服务,管理半径大、运营难度高。

要想解决以上问题,必须把消费者、服务者、经营者放在一个系统里来协调升级。为此,2019年悦管家提出了蝴蝶型商业模式——通过效率革命,打造出一个消费者、服务者、悦管家共赢的生态圈。

刘珺认为家政行业服务效率、匹配效率、沟通效率低下。提升效率首先要提升服务者对服务业和悦管家的认同感。通过从收入、成长、尊重这三个服务者最关心的维度真正理解和培养服务者,才能够保证团队的稳定及不断成长。悦管家通过对招聘—培训—上岗—晋升的服务者职业全生命周期进行深入分析和设计,不断增强服务者对家政服务的认同感。

随着时代的发展，年轻群体逐渐成为社会上的主力消费群体。在科技飞速发展、生活节奏逐步加快的环境下，他们的生活结构、生活习惯等都发生了巨大的变化，时间变得越发碎片化，为了匹配这种变化，生活服务提供方也必须提供具备碎片化、个性化的产品及组织形态。

由于家庭结构与以前不同，且现在的年轻人常有较大的生活压力，这导致他们习惯于将生活服务类需求进行外包。同时，现在是消费者主权时代，消费者倾向于根据自己的意愿及偏好去市场上选购所需的商品和服务。而在互联网时代，要想通过信息不对称去赚取利润，绝对不是企业长远发展的方向与路径。刘珺坚信只有让消费者从内心认同企业提供的商品或服务，真正给消费者带来便利的商品及服务，才能够真正把握住市场。

悦管家从服务的安全性（放心）、服务的便利性（省心）、服务的品质及体验（舒心）这三个关键点出发，深入挖掘消费者的需求，对每个关键点进行设计，力争全方位满足消费者的需求。

消费者与服务者之间无法形成有效链接的主要原因在于信任体系的缺失。消费者认为服务提供方的实际成本远远低于消费者支付的价格；服务提供方认为消费者支付的价格与服务品质无法匹配；更复杂的是，服务提供方又分为实际服务者与服务匹配平台，而实际服务者又认为平台在中间抽取的利润远远大于平台实际付出的成本，这就导致服务行业特有的"跳单"行为不断发生。为了平衡三方的顾虑，悦管家致力于打造服务业信任体系，通过科技与企业管理流程的革新，不断提高服务提供方的效率，降低服务成本。

悦管家的效率平台是连接消费者与服务者的连接器，也是悦管家蝴蝶型商业模式的核心。悦管家利用互联网技术，建立了共享服务平台，整合社会化服务者资源，为家庭和企业提供卓越的服务品质和体验，降低消费者和服务者之间的沟通成本，实现消费者、服务者和悦管家的三赢局面。悦管家还成立了专门的技术研发团队，自主研发业务系统，不断对平台进行打磨，力求达到效率的最大化。

在服务效率方面，悦管家通过打造家政服务行业的高学历、年轻化的服务者团队，引导队伍在时刻保持工作激情的同时，自发地去提高工作效率。在匹配效率方面，悦管家开发的自动派单系统具备了规则引擎计算得分进行派单、高星级或高技能服务者优先、长期固定用户分配优先、用户偏好数据优化、服务者路径数据优化、大数据不断优化推荐效率等一系列提升派单效率及匹配度的功能。在沟通效率方面，悦管家以线上线下全渠道（微信、PC、App、电话）服务下单的开放平台，结合24小时在线管家、服务者自动背景调查审核的企业信任背书与0延时反馈，确保了消费者与服务者、消费者与悦管家、悦管家与服务者之间沟通效率的最大化。

（资料来源：根据网络资料整理）

案例思考题：

1. 请绘制出悦管家商业模式在各个阶段的商业模式画布。
2. 你认为悦管家商业模式迭代四阶段分别存在什么样的价值创造逻辑？

分析提示：

1. 商业模式画布由以下要素组成：客户细分、价值主张、渠道通路、关键业务、收入来源、核心资源、成本结构、重要合作及客户关系。从模式1.0到模式4.0，悦管家的商业模式画布在每一阶段都发生了一些变化，可以从以上要素对各个阶段进行分析。

2. 商业模式创造价值的逻辑性表现在以下方面：价值发现、价值匹配和价值获取。每个阶段悦管家的价值创造逻辑都不相同。

案例 *13*

用社会创业实现精准扶贫：龙游飞鸡

知识点：

社会创业定义、社会创业与商业创业区别、社会创业机会识别过程、合法性。

案例目的：

通过"龙游飞鸡"创业项目的学习，使学生认识社会创业这一创业形式，了解社会创业与商业创业的区别，掌握社会创业过程中的合法性策略。

案例正文：

1. 初识龙游麻鸡

陈永军一直从事商业模式设计、文化创新、品牌设计等工作，经营着一家互联网公司和一家文化公司，在公司经营方面积累了丰富的经验。

2016年5月，陈永军在陪朋友胡潇文回老家浙江省龙游县探亲的时候，受到了龙游当地麻鸡的的吸引。陈永军了解到龙游麻鸡虽然品质好，但是销路却一直不好，当地农户日子贫苦。陈永军想要改变现状，带领农户增收致富，于是他开始着手帮农户卖鸡。

市面上常见的都是饲料喂养的鸡，但龙游麻鸡却不一样，它们被放养在山林中，产蛋率高，产的蛋质量好，1973年就已开始出口，2013年被列入了浙江省畜禽遗传资源保护名录。

陈永军通过调研发现，龙游麻鸡卖不出去的原因是：龙游麻鸡是龙游本地的传统鸡种，在龙游以外的地区没有形成口碑，消费人群少；而且养殖农户大多分布在偏远的山区，交通不便。散养在山林的土鸡虽深受城里人的追捧，但想找到真正的土鸡却并不容易。陈永军发现土鸡市场良莠不齐，有不少商贩用以饲料喂养的鸡来冒充散养土鸡。陈永军认为，打通销售渠道是扭转局势的关键，贫困农户应该改变原有的销售方式，主动出击。

由于市面上土鸡同质化严重，因此陈永军为龙游麻鸡取名为"龙游飞鸡"。他通过微信公众号"龙游飞鸡"搭建垂直电商平台，在农村土特产品与都市消费者之间架起了销售的桥梁。之后，他说服胡潇文加入团队中。

2016年12月2日，电商平台正式上线。为了改变过去无包装、无品牌、无规范的状况，陈永军和胡潇文从宰杀到包装、销售、物流的整个过程都制定了严格的标准，保障了飞鸡质量的稳定性、安全性和规范性。同时两人利用过去积累的人脉资源广泛宣传，使原本滞销的龙游麻鸡被抢购一空。

2. 带领农户养鸡

最初的目的已经达成，陈永军和胡潇文本来已经可以回到原来的生活，但看到需要帮助的农户，他们决定留下来一起养鸡，他们的决定遭到了家人和朋友的反对和误解，但他们并没有因为外界的否定而放弃。2017年12月，龙游宗泰农产品有限公司（以下简称龙游宗泰）正式成立，公司以"人人有事做，家家有收入"为愿景，致力于带领农户脱贫增收。

为了打消农户的疑虑，两人提出了"三免两保"的承诺。三免，即免费提供2个月成熟鸡种，以提高鸡苗成活率；免费搭建鸡棚、围栏等配套设施，帮农户做好前期准备工作；免费接入网线，安装实时物联网系统监控设备。两保，即签订回购协议，保证按照市场价收购鸡和鸡蛋；为龙游飞鸡购买养殖保险。

两人先说服已经退休的老村主任养鸡。有了老村主任的示范，许多农户也纷纷跟着加入。两人还积极与政府部门对接，表达帮农户脱贫的想法。政府的很多领导先后多次与他们交谈，并深入考察了"龙游飞鸡"项目，帮助他们对接媒体资源，并向当地贫困户鼎力推荐。在政府的大力推广下，新华社、中央电视台、人民网、浙江卫视、浙江日报等各大主流媒体都争相报道"龙游飞鸡"。

2018年9月，"龙游飞鸡"扶贫模式成功复制到四川省泸州市叙永县和广西壮族自治区巴马县。据统计，2018年"龙游飞鸡"项目共带动700多户农户一起养鸡致富。

"三免两保"的实施为"龙游飞鸡"项目打开了局面。为了进一步发掘该项目的潜力，更好地帮助农户致富，陈永军制定了以下方案。

（1）贫困户优先

为了帮助这些低收入农户精准脱贫，陈永军决定，"龙游飞鸡"项目优先选取残疾人家庭、低收入家庭、偏远山区留守人群和山地种植农户作为指定合作农户。为了在保证这些农户利益不受损害的同时，又能保证鸡的养殖质量，陈永军设立了统一的养殖标准，极大提升了农户养殖的质量与效益。

（2）金融联未来

针对农户没有资产，很难在银行贷款的问题，陈永军提出由龙游宗泰与衢州龙游农商银行签订战略合作协议，银行根据养殖收益为农户提供相应的资金借贷和农业金融服务。

（3）合作经薄村

鸡种是否纯正，是"龙游飞鸡"能否持续占领市场的关键。但龙游宗泰与农户合作以来，鸡苗一直是委托外部种源场进行培育，不仅合作成本很高，品质也难以保证。为此，陈永军决定建立能够自己控制成本和质量的种源场。经过考察，陈永军发现，龙游县内有几个村适合孵养鸡苗。建立种源场，不但能保证鸡种品质，更能带动这几个村集体增收。在红利分配方式上，陈永军充分考虑村集体增收的迫切需要，选择了见效最快的方式：种源场每出栏一只健康鸡苗，村集体就能收到2元的现金收入。

3. 飞进千家万户

"龙游飞鸡"能否成功，市场与客户的选择至关重要。在最开始帮农户卖鸡的时候，陈永军的目标客户就是对绿色食品有需求，有消费能力的城市消费群体。

那么，如何吸引消费者购买"龙游飞鸡"呢？第一，要使消费者信任绿色食品的品质。通过实时直播农户养殖场景，加深消费者对"龙游飞鸡"原生态、真实性的信任。

第二，用真实的农村场景和农户生活状况，唤起消费者想要改变农村落后现状的情感。陈永军在微信平台中发布了"农民创客"系列纪录片，该记录片记录了农户养殖"龙游飞鸡"以来的巨大改变。通过农户的现身说法和养殖场景，让消费者切实感受到，购买"龙游飞鸡"确确实实能够帮助农户获得收入、改善生活。

龙游宗泰的企业使命为："用一只鸡养活一家人，让一枚蛋供起大学生"，"龙游飞鸡"向消费者传递了"人人有事做、家家有收入"的愿景和情怀。为了扩大产品的知名度，陈永军发展了两条销售路线：线上，建立"龙游飞鸡"微信群；线下，搭建别致场景，邀请客户实地体验。

2021年，"龙游飞鸡"启动了"百城联百农、千企系千村"农民增收活动，与浙江省"千企结千村、消灭薄弱村"专项行动精准吻合、无缝对接。龙游飞鸡的这次活动，为企业和农户带来了可持续的双赢局面。

案例思考题：

1. 陈永军为什么创办"龙游飞鸡"项目？
2. "龙游飞鸡"项目与一般的商业项目有何不同？
3. 陈永军是如何克服"龙游飞鸡"项目启动时的困难，最终赢得社会认可的？

分析提示：

1. 商业创业的动机大多是利己的（如追求个人财富），而社会创业的动机大多是利他的（如追求社会公平）。社会创业机会识别过程包含三个阶段：社会创业机会感知、社会创业机会发现与社会创业机会创造。本题需将社会创业动机和社会创业机会识别过程结合起来进行分析。

2. 商业创业与社会创业是两种不同类型的创业活动。从创业动机看，商业创业以利己动机为主导，社会创业以利他动机为主导；从创业机会来源看，商业创业机会通常来源于待解决的市场问题，而社会创业机会通常来源于待解决的社会问题；从创业目标看，商业创业以创造经济价值为目标，社会创业以创造社会价值为目标。本题可从创业动机、创业机会来源和创业目标进行比较分析。

3. 合法性对创业活动的开展至关重要，具备合法性的创业活动更容易获得资源以及持续的支持。由于社会创业往往需要用创新的手段解决社会问题，所以社会创业也会面临一些合法性挑战，此时就需要采取一些策略促进社会创业合法性的形成。合法性可以分为规制合法性、规范合法性及认知合法性。本题可从以上角度，分析"龙游飞鸡"项目获取合法性的具体措施。

案例 14

创业传承：海伦钢琴

知识点：

家族创业、代际目标。

案例目的：

本案例以海伦家族传承为背景，主要讲述海伦钢琴传承创业的过程，使学生了解家族企业传承创业中家族目标的形成过程；了解代际家庭互动如何促进代际目标的兼容性；理解代际目标相容性对家族企业传承和创业的促进。

案例正文：

2019年1月28日，在中央广播电视台播出的春晚中，有70多台海伦钢琴及数名由海伦钢琴选送的演奏者参与了《我爱你中国》节目的录制。事实上，这并不是海伦钢琴第一次受到公众的关注。早在2008年，海伦钢琴就曾被选为北京奥运系列演出用琴，并受到欧洲领先音乐杂志的高度评价。如今，海伦钢琴股份有限公司（以下简称海伦钢琴）已成为国家文化输出重点企业，其产品产销量位居世界前列。作为一家民营企业，海伦钢琴经历了从无到有，从配件生产到整机生产，从制造业到服务业的完整转型升级。

1. 行业背景及企业现状

钢琴生产在国外已有数百年的历史，但在中国的发展历史并不长。近年来，经济的快速发展推动了钢琴在中国家庭中的普及。中国钢琴产业市场规模在2018年达到1003亿元；2019年达到1042亿元。其中，电钢琴市场规模也不断增长，2022年，中国电钢琴市场规模达到79亿元，预计2025年将增长至100亿元。同时，促进钢琴产业发展的政策不断出台，为钢琴行业发展提供政策支持。

海伦钢琴成立于2001年，主要从事钢琴制造、乐器产品、汽车配件等业务，注册资本2.54亿元，是国家重点火炬计划实施高新技术企业，国家重点文化出口企业。

作为"中国驰名商标",海伦钢琴生产的立式钢琴、三角钢琴在世界范围内得到广泛认可和赞誉,公司产品远销欧美、日本等地。海伦钢琴在欧洲、北美有近 300 条钢琴线代理销售海伦钢琴产品,在日本有 40 多条钢琴线,全球共 800 多条钢琴线。

基于智能钢琴的教育培训是海伦钢琴的新兴业务,线上线下艺术教育业务融合,形成海伦钢琴新的竞争优势。2019 年,海伦钢琴与中央音乐学院、海伦继续教育学院共同开发海伦智能项目。由中央音乐学院开发教材,海伦钢琴在世界各地进行师资培训与指导,以教学效果和艺术特色为轴心开展钢琴教学工作,开启了艺术教育与钢琴教学的新纪元。

2. 一代人的建设:从硬件代码到整个仪器制造

海伦钢琴成立前,陈海伦经营着一家五金配件厂,主要业务是为国内钢琴企业提供配件。当时的钢琴市场主要被广东珠江、上海施特劳斯、辽宁诺迪斯卡、北京星海四大品牌占领,竞争非常激烈。陈海伦梦想将工厂带到一个新的平台,他把目光投向了钢琴的"引擎"——核心部件"码克"。这就意味着企业要升级主导产品,提高技术和工艺,打造高品质、高品位的生产线,人才、技术和制造工具成为迫在眉睫的问题。幸运的是,当时的北京星海公司和奥地利文德龙公司为海伦钢琴提供了先进的技术支持。此外,陈海伦还斥巨资从日本进口了先进的五轴联动设备。2001—2002 年,海伦钢琴完成了设备升级。2003 年 3 月,在德国法兰克福展会上,陈海伦向世界展示了他的"码克"产品。产品一经展出,就受到国外厂商的追捧。正是在这次展会上,陈海伦深刻意识到技术人员的重要性。此后,陈海伦以重金聘请专家指导他的工厂,甚至用当时海伦钢琴年利润的一半来支付人才佣金。

从配件到整机的生产转变,对海伦来说是一场革命。乘着"码克"研制成功的东风,海伦钢琴创办了钢琴制造工程技术研究中心,将公司年营业收入的 5% 投入钢琴制造技术研发,并注册了"HAILUN"钢琴商标,开始研制自主品牌钢琴。为了避免与国内老牌厂商的竞争和资金来源的流失,陈海伦采取了以配件养琴的策略——将生产的钢琴全部销往欧洲,不进入国内市场。2003 年,海伦钢琴首台立式钢琴研制成功。2004 年,海伦钢琴生产的 500 台立式钢琴全部销往欧洲市场;2005

年，海伦钢琴放弃钢琴配件业务，集中资源生产自主品牌钢琴，并开拓国内市场，当年售出560台HG178三角钢琴。2019年，海伦钢琴年销量达到10.5万台，位居全球第四，并于2012年在深交所正式挂牌。

3. 父子齐心协力：从整机制造到智能钢琴

海伦钢琴一代人确立的"慢而稳"的发展理念也深刻影响了二代人的目标塑造。2010年，陈海伦的独子陈朝峰加入海伦钢琴。进入海伦钢琴后，陈朝峰先是在工厂车间轮岗，由此对整个钢琴生产过程有了初步的了解；之后，他负责IPO和对外投资。通过总结和学习，陈朝峰的个人能力得到了快速提升。自2012年公司上市以来，智能钢琴的研发就被提上了日程，2013年，陈朝峰开始负责智能钢琴的研发。

海伦钢琴虽然在传统钢琴制造中已处于行业领先地位，但在智能技术领域还是新手。在与北京邮电大学合作失败后，海伦钢琴开始走自主研发道路。海伦钢琴一方面借鉴欧美的先进经验，开始在音频同步、电流噪声等方面进行深入挖掘；另一方面，在音频同步的支持下，不断完善远程音乐交流功能。4G和5G网络的发展，使得远程传输更加精准。海伦钢琴利用网络更新使远程音乐同步传输，满足了智能钢琴的音质要求，由此音质无损成为其智能钢琴的优势。此外，自动演奏功能也成为智能钢琴的优势，即当一方在线播放歌曲时，另一方便可通过智能钢琴再现该歌曲的演奏，强度和键序统一，便于教师指导学生学习，还适用于实时远程音乐培训。但该技术尚不成熟。例如，在表演连续性方面，由于自动表演是靠电力驱动的，而且电池会发烫，因此智能钢琴很难长时间保持发音的精准度。2014年，随着智能钢琴的研发，海伦钢琴成立全资子公司"北京海伦网络信息技术有限公司"，为母公司提供信息技术支持。

4. 第二代领先：从智能钢琴到培训学校

2014年，陈朝峰创立了"海伦艺术教育投资有限公司"，研究海伦钢琴从制造到服务的艺术教育产业。陈氏父子认为，中国艺术教育培训市场还存在差距，智能钢琴不仅具有便捷的娱乐功能，还可以用于钢琴教学。因此，海伦钢琴建立音乐培训学校，进入艺术教育市场。中国艺术启蒙教育市场的空白，让智能钢琴有了一席之地。

智能钢琴为海伦钢琴的教育培训奠定了基础。陈朝峰的团队开发了一款 App，实现一对多的教学与培训，不仅降低了家长的成本，还让孩子在学习过程中能够相互交流，并通过动画的方式激发孩子的学习兴趣。海伦钢琴通过按键指示灯对孩子进行纠错指导，通过软件对孩子进行伙伴式训练，从而为孩子提供私人辅导。海伦钢琴也在积极设计自己的课程，聘请北京师范大学的教授指导课程的设计，并将其应用于网络教学的软件中，钢琴教室、音乐培训学校和智力培训学校也在逐步建立中。海伦钢琴还与宁波大学合作，率先成立试点音乐学校，并成功与中央音乐学院签约，共同开发课程内容。

海伦家族两代人的努力，推动了海伦钢琴从一个小小的钢琴配件厂发展成行业龙头企业。在发展过程中，海伦钢琴不仅实现了企业的转型发展，还顺利完成了家族传承。父子共治让两代人顺利完成更替，家族二代也在创业经历中成长为优秀的接班人。

案例思考题：

1. 在跨代传承过程中，家族企业内涌现出哪些多元化的创业目标？目标设定的主体有哪些？
2. 家族两代领导者之间的互动如何影响多元化的家族企业目标兼容？
3. 为什么两代领导者的目标兼容能在传承过程中促进家族企业的转型？

分析提示：

1. 家族企业是由两代领导者共同主导的企业实体，其目标在跨代传承的情境中产生变化。领导者是目标设定的主体，理解不同主体在目标设定的动机方面的差异，有助于家族企业理解多元目标差异。

2. 家族企业的目标兼容与企业发展和家族传承同步进行，其中代际互动对调整家族成员动机具有重要作用。建议采用家庭科学理论和社会情感财富理论，分析代际互动在目标兼容过程中的作用。

3. 传统企业转型是家族企业一代领导者逐步移交权力的过程，也是二代领导者创业能力的展现过程。在家族企业中，二代领导者创业能力的展现需要在一代领导者的合作下才能得以完成，可使用目标理论分析传承目标和创业目标如何在代际情境下实现。

Case 1

Taobao, Pinduoduo, and Ningda Yunchuang Town

Key Points:

Entrepreneurial types; Entrepreneurial logic; Entrepreneurship; Innovation

Case Purpose:

Through the brief introduction of three cases of Taobao, Pinduoduo, and Yunchuang Town, this section aims to help students master the types and logic of entrepreneurship, and understand the differences and connections between entrepreneurship and innovation.

Case Description:

Taobao

Taobao is a popular online shopping and retail platform in China, with nearly 500 million registered users. It attracts over 60 million daily visitors and has more than 800 million listed products. On average, 48,000 items are sold every minute.

In 2003, when public awareness of online shopping and the internet was limited, Ma Yun founded Taobao to explore the C2C (Consumer-to-Consumer) model in China. In 2007, Taobao became the largest retail website in Asia, with an annual transaction volume exceeding 40 billion yuan, making it the second-largest comprehensive department store in China. Currently, Taobao has evolved from a single C2C model to a comprehensive retail ecosystem that includes C2C, group buying, distribution, auctions, and other e-commerce models. It has become one of the global platforms for e-commerce transactions.

Pinduoduo

Pinduoduo is a third-party social e-commerce platform focusing on C2M (Consumer-to-Manufacturer) group shopping. It was established in September 2015. Users can purchase products at lower prices by initiating group purchases with friends and family. The platform aims to harness the power of collective buying to provide people with greater benefits and fun. Pinduoduo's unique social e-commerce thinking is based on the concept of communication and sharing.

In 2019, Pinduoduo was selected as one of the "100 Exemplary Brands" at the 2019 China Brand Power Summit. In 2020, it ranked 1649th on the Forbes Global 2000 list. Positioned between Taobao and JD.com, Pinduoduo has achieved strong growth and has established itself as a platform where "everything can be found at a lower price at Pinduoduo".

Ningbo University Yunchuang Town

Ningbo University Yunchuang 1986 Youth Town (Yunchuang Town), formerly known as the East Gate Commercial Street of Ningbo University, opened on October 1, 2016. Yunchuang Town brings together various business formats, including dining, retail, leisure, and education, and encompasses entrepreneurship, cultural exchange, and lifestyle. With community elements such as tourism, culture, art leisure, gourmet food, trendy entertainment, and maker apartments, the town has created a young community with a self-sustaining ecosystem.

Currently, stores in Yunchuang Town include Starbucks, Kentucky Fried Chicken, Iron Paste Pizza, Tangdao Soup, Big Pot Food, Liubenmu Daily Food, Huili, Zui Internet Cafe, Sihe Internet Garden, Baodao Glasses, CGV Bright Glasses, Bojia, Lawson, Owen, Yidiandian.

Questions:

1. Do you consider Ma Yun's entrepreneurship to be opportunity-based or necessity-based? Which kind of entrepreneurial type does each store in Yunchuang Town fall under?

2. Did Ma Yun's creation of Taobao follow causal logic or effectual logic?

3. Whether it is Taobao, Pinduoduo, or Yunchuang Town, they all gather a large number of businesses. Please evaluate them from an innovative perspective and explain the relationship between entrepreneurship and innovation.

Case Analysis:

1. Entrepreneurship types vary, and survival entrepreneurship and opportunity entrepreneurship are two common types in China. Survival entrepreneurship is motivated by the lack of other options, where entrepreneurs have no choice but to solve their difficulties through entrepreneurship. On the other hand, opportunity entrepreneurship is driven by a strong desire to seize existing opportunities and create value.

2. Causal logic and effectual logic are commonly used entrepreneurial logics. Causal logic is goal-oriented, while effectual logic is means-oriented.

3. Entrepreneurship does not necessarily equal innovation, and innovation does not always lead to entrepreneurship. However, entrepreneurship based on innovation tends to have a higher chance of success. Taobao's entrepreneurship is more innovative, while Pinduoduo and Ningbo University Yunchuang Town are not highly innovative overall. Although all three involve entrepreneurial activities, they differ in terms of innovativeness.

Case 2

The Entrepreneurship of Shanghai Haiting Environmental Engineering Co., Ltd.

Key Points:

Entrepreneurial preparation; Entrepreneurial skills; Entrepreneurial team; Entrepreneurial mindset

Case Purpose:

Through the analysis of a college students' entrepreneurship case, this section aims to help students understand the common problems faced by college students in the entrepreneurial process and the key decisions in entrepreneurship, and emphasizes the importance of entrepreneurial preparation.

Case Description:

Zhang Xuanjun was admitted to Hunan University in 1994 to study chemical industrial engineering. After graduating with a bachelor's degree, he worked at Visteon Guangzhou Branch and Dongguan Maolin Electronics Co., Ltd. While working, Zhang Xuanjun realized that he had many deficiencies in professional knowledge and management skills. As a result, he decided to resign and pursue further studies. In 2001, he entered Xiangtan University to pursue a master's degree in environmental engineering. Later, he entered Tongji University to pursue a Ph.D. in environmental science.

During his doctoral study, Zhang Xuanjun accumulated practical experience while engaging in academic research. He has served as a project manager in Shanghai Keyu Water Treatment Technology Co., Ltd and Shanghai Wanhong Environmental Technology Co., Ltd. In May 2007, he chose to start his own business and founded Shanghai Haiting Environmental Engineering Co., Ltd.

Zhang Xuanjun had long-held aspirations for entrepreneurship. During his university years, he actively participated in social practice activities and gained practical experience through work as a mall promoter and company salesperson. These experiences made Zhang Xuanjun realize the importance of execution. He began to assemble his team to implement smaller entrepreneurial projects, such as selling baby products, which earned him a profit of 60,000 yuan in just three days. Later, he seized various market opportunities, such as selling second-hand bicycles, motorcycles, digital products, and acting as an agent for credit cards and SIM cards. After graduation, Zhang Xuanjun chose to work in a company mainly based on three considerations: First, the business activities he engaged in during university were still far from true entrepreneurship. Second, his risk tolerance was relatively weak right after graduation. Finally, working could accumulate some experience and networks, laying the foundation for future entrepreneurship.

In 2005, Zhang Xuanjun's doctoral research project became the core research content of the scientific research plan project "Research on New Technologies and Mathematical Models for Anaerobic Treatment of Urban Sewage" of the Shanghai Science and Technology Commission, and was supported by the national "Tenth Five Year" and "Eleventh Five Year" science and technology research projects. Under the guidance of his tutor, Zhang Xuanjun and his project members worked hard for more than a year and finally achieved a technological breakthrough by developing a new type of external circulation anaerobic reactor and applying for a national patent. The reactor has many advantages in wastewater treatment, such as simple structure, low energy consumption, integrated treatment of multiple pollutants, water quality compliance, and easy management.

Subsequently, the new external circulation anaerobic reactor was applied in many wastewater treatment plants in Jiangsu. Due to its excellent performance, it received unanimous praise from companies. The research team reached initial agreements on equipment promotion with companies in Kunshan and Changzhou. With the strong support of his tutor, Zhang Xuanjun established Shanghai Haiting Environmental Engineering Co., Ltd. (hereinafter referred to as Haiting) in May 2007.Zhang Xuanjun received a sponsorship of 200,000 yuan from the Tongji University Student Entrepreneurship Fund and a loan of 200,000 yuan from his tutor. His team member Liu Hongbo also joined the team. Haiting officially began operations in 2007.

At the beginning of his entrepreneurship, Zhang Xuanjun encountered many difficulties. In the first six months of its establishment, Haiting did not receive any business orders and was in a pure "burning money" stage, resulting in the rapid depletion of the raised funds. Zhang Xuanjun then sought a change in business philosophy, requiring all company members to go out and explore the market. He also changed the business strategy, not only promoting their own products but also acting as an agent for other products and providing technical consulting services. Through these changes in business philosophy and strategy, the company gradually improved, undertook projects of various sizes, and established cooperative relationships with customers.

After surviving the difficult initial period, Haiting entered a phase of rapid development. On one hand, it continued to expand cooperation with various technology companies, jointly undertaking projects, and supporting and complementing each other in terms of technology and products. On the other hand, it actively sought opportunities to promote its core products and cooperated with market-oriented companies, using sales agency methods to expand its business. This reduced Haiting's operating costs and risks, leading to a rapid increase in overall revenue. With the continuous expansion of business, Haiting's reputation continued to grow, laying a solid foundation for its future development. In 2009, Haiting's sales reached 35 million yuan, an increase of 26 million yuan compared to 2008.

One factor constraining Haiting's rapid development was the lack of professional managers. At the beginning of Haiting's establishment, the business mainly consisted of small projects, and the annual turnover was relatively low, so the problem was not significant. However, after entering a phase of rapid development, this problem became apparent. For example, for projects with large amounts of money, payment was usually made in installments. Setting the payment dates and balancing monthly financial reports was a critical issue. Due to a lack of financial management talent in the company, there were often a large number of project payments in the same month, resulting in the payment of a large amount of taxes in that month, while other months had little or no income. Moreover, as the business volume, sales, and number of company employees continued to increase, the free and casual management approach was no longer suitable for Haiting's rapid development. Insufficient understanding of scientific management in the early stages of operation resulted in many losses for Haiting.

Another factor constraining Haiting's rapid development was capital. Although Haiting's annual sales reached millions of yuan, the actual cash available for free use was limited. With the increase in project amounts, more funds were needed for project operations. Zhang Xuanjun considered various solutions to the funding problem, but none were ideal. Since Haiting had nothing to mortgage and could not find suitable people to guarantee loans, it could not obtain bank loans. Private short-term loans had high interest rates and high risks. In the prevailing policy environment, it was difficult for Haiting to apply for project funds. Since most of Haiting's sales came from traditional business, and the sales of core products were not ideal, venture capital firms were not willing to take the risk. Unable to find sufficient financial support, Haiting could only cooperate with larger companies to jointly undertake large projects. However, cooperation meant a decrease in profits, and the company's assets could not grow rapidly.

Haiting's development relied heavily on other companies. On the one hand, Haiting had a relatively narrow product line and limited service scope, and many projects required collaboration with other companies. On the other hand, due to a lack of relevant industry qualifications, some projects had to be hosted by other companies, and Haiting did not yet have the conditions to operate independently. In addition, Haiting primarily focused on technology, products, and service output, and used cooperation with other companies and sales agency implementation to expand its business. It lacked its own market development team, making it difficult to control annual sales performance and expand the market in a planned and systematic manner.

Questions:

1. What do you think are the key factors for the success of college student entrepreneurship?

2. Why was Zhang Xuanjun able to lead Haiting to rapid development in the early stages of entrepreneurship ? Why did he encounter so many problems later?

3. Are the problems encountered by Haiting in its development unavoidable? How can they be prevented in advance?

Case Analysis:

1. Entrepreneurship often faces failure, so adequate preparation is necessary before starting a business, including knowledge, skills, practical experience, etc. Since college students lack extensive social experience, their entrepreneurial behavior often exhibits strong impulsiveness, and they tend to overlook preparation, market research, and policy and legal aspects.

2. Entrepreneurial preparation has a significant impact on early entrepreneurial success. However, as the company grows and faces a complex internal and external environment, the entrepreneur's early preparation may not be sufficient to support the company's development.

3. Since entrepreneurship involves various problems, such as lack of funds and team conflicts, entrepreneurs should adopt a mindset of using the uncertain environment to create opportunities. For example, entrepreneurs need to continuously learn about entrepreneurship, focus on team building and organizational development, take swift actions, iterate and learn from failures, and quickly find viable business models.

Case 3

Three Entrepreneurship Stories

Key Points:

Qualities of entrepreneurs; Whether entrepreneurs are born or made; Entrepreneurial preparation

Case Purpose:

Entrepreneurship is a challenging journey. If one relies solely on passion without preparation, that path becomes a dead end. Therefore, this case is designed to be inspiring and open-ended, mainly to stimulate students' thinking about. (1) What preparations are needed for entrepreneurship; (2) Self-assessment of suitability for entrepreneurship.

Case Description:

Awen's Big Wardrobe

Desiring to have a big wardrobe filled with beautiful clothes and share the sense of beauty with her sisters, Awen, a "post-80s" girl, had the initial intention of starting her own business. Five years ago, after graduating from college, Awen had been engaged in design work related to her profession, living the typical nine-to-five life of a white-collar worker. However, the dream of a big wardrobe had prompted her to take the first step in entrepreneurship.

Before opening her clothing store, Awen knew nothing about running a business, apart from selecting clothes. She had to start from scratch, whether it was the store's decoration style, hospitality, or pricing of clothes. Awen believed that starting a business was difficult, and many small details of operations had to be explored and accumulated by oneself. For example, considering the factors of the market itself and the impact of communication, not even one of Awen's preferred store names was used in the end.

Awen was lucky that no major mistakes occurred since the store's opening, and there were no unpleasant disputes with customers. She believed it was because she had spent a lot of time behind the scenes, paying attention to the easily overlooked details. Every piece of clothing in Awen's store was carefully selected by her, and she felt happy to see these beautiful clothes worn by the right people. To this day, Awen continues to do her own design work while managing the clothing store, and she prefers to see the place as a space for communication with like-minded people.

Regarding entrepreneurship, Awen believes that many people around her have a dream of starting their own business but have not taken the first step due to various reasons.

Jiajia's Board Game Store

Jiajia, who had plans for entrepreneurship after graduating from university, only opened the door to entrepreneurship when he accidentally came across a board role-play game called "Three Kingdoms" in 2009.

At that time, "Three Kingdoms" was not popular yet, and board games were not well known either. Jiajia thought that board games had simple environmental and equipment requirements, were not only environmentally friendly and healthy but could also enhance communication among friends, which was indeed a good game.

Later, he learned that board games had been popular in Europe and America for decades but were just beginning to rise in China. Therefore, he and his partner chose a board game store as their "first stop" for entrepreneurship. On the one hand, it was due to a lack of funds, and on the other hand, they did not conduct market research at that time, so they were unsure if board games would be accepted by the local consumers.

In July 2009, Jiajia began preparations for opening the store. He visited similar stores in major cities, found sources for board games, learned about the gameplay of large-scale board games, and designed a pricing model. Two months later, the board game store officially opened.

At the beginning, there was a continuous flow of customers, exceeding Jiajia's expectations. However, he soon discovered many problems in the store, such as poor soundproofing causing interference between customers and insufficient manpower leading to poor service quality. The high prices also deterred many people from participating. Eventually, Jiajia and his partner decided to increase staff and revise the pricing model, gradually attracting a group of loyal customers.

Meng Yan's 7 Months of Entrepreneurship

Meng Yan studied business management at university and worked for a year in a company selling bearings after graduation. Due to constantly being in the market, interacting with clients, Meng Yan quickly acquired knowledge and skills in this area, fueling his desire to start a business.

He learned that his classmate, Xiao Xie, had family members engaged in mechanical bearing sales and earned a good income. Xiao Xie also had relevant work experience and some client resources. Meng Yan decided to work together with Xiao Xie. Their entrepreneurial goals were clear: to lay the foundation for the future and earn more money. However, they were not experts in how to operate, the current market prospects, the characteristics of the industry, or the performance of the products.

In April 2002, Meng Yan borrowed 50,000 yuan, and Xiao Xie borrowed over 30,000 yuan for the purpose of starting a business. Over the next two months, Meng Yan and Xiao Xie moved to the company premises to live. During the day, they prepared envelopes containing quotation sheets and other materials to be sent to various enterprises. After sending out tens of thousands of letters, they received no business inquiries but instead received mail returned from the post office every day. However, the two of them did not lose heart. In August 2002, they began visiting various machinery equipment and bearing exhibitions, distributing materials to visiting merchants, and contacting manufacturers. This method allowed them to collect hundreds of business cards from intermediaries, including both domestic and foreign buyers. They felt excited about this situation, as they believed the prospects were becoming brighter.

Meng Yan and Xiao Xie input the collected business cards into the computer to make a database. With the follow-up effect of the exhibitions, they received dozens of calls or business inquiries every day. Over a month later, Meng Yan noticed that something was amiss. Although customers came to inquire every day, there were few follow-ups. Meng Yan and Xiao Xie became anxious and sought advice from industry insiders. These insiders believed that the situation in the mechanical bearing industry was complex, and as it had developed, the relationships between domestic and foreign manufacturers and suppliers had become relatively stable. Therefore, having good product quality and low prices did not necessarily guarantee attracting customers.

Meng Yan wanted to become proactive and increase direct communication with customers through on-site visits. He mobilized all his classmates, friends, and family members to help him find acquaintances in related companies, but the results were minimal. Meng Yan decided to hire a few salespeople and drafted a sales plan. This meant increasing monthly expenses by at least 2,000 to 3,000 yuan.

After hiring the salespeople for over two months, the company still didn't make any money, and Meng Yan became even more anxious. Shortly before the National Day holiday, Meng Yan received the first business order, with a contract value of over 70,000 yuan and a profit of just over 4,000 yuan. The company subsequently signed several small orders, earning less than 10,000 yuan. Afterward, the company's business improved, establishing a good reputation, and attracting more and more customers. Although the orders were all small, the profits barely covered their monthly expenses.

However, the temporary success could not hide the deficiencies in the company's system and Meng Yan's lack of entrepreneurship skills. The company's organizational structure and framework were inherently problematic, coupled with confusion in accounting and employee work order. Troubles quickly arose. The salespeople engaged in internal competition, sabotaging each other to gain clients. Initially, Meng Yan didn't pay much attention to this, but things gradually worsened. One salesperson went as far as conducting private transactions with manufacturers to seize orders. When supply problems occurred, the manufacturer approached Meng Yan for compensation, but that salesperson had already left. To protect the company's reputation, Meng Yan had to provide some compensation, wiping out two months of profits. Moreover, the intense competition among the company's salespeople became widely known within the industry. Manufacturers became suspicious, and the company's business once again fell into a deadlock.

In November, Xiao Xie proposed to dissolve the partnership and took away client information. Meng Yan's business was completely in dire straits. The ship that had just set sail ran aground like this. Meng Yan concluded that he should have worked at a foreign trade company for two to three years first, accumulating experience and client resources before embarking on entrepreneurship.

Questions:

1. Based on the above three cases, what qualities and abilities do you think entrepreneurs should possess in general?

2. What preparations should be made for entrepreneurship?

Case Analysis:

1. Awen's case tells us that entrepreneurship requires the drive to pursue dreams, perseverance, and courage. Jiajia's case highlights the importance of market research before starting a business. Meng Yan's case shows that entrepreneurship requires both passion and corresponding skills for success. Entrepreneurs generally need qualities such as passion, alertness, risk-taking, and innovation.

2. Entrepreneurship is a difficult journey. Without adequate preparation, relying solely on passion will lead to a dead end. Preparations for entrepreneurship should include personnel, funding, market research, knowledge, and experience accumulation, among others.

Case 4

The Failure of Company D

Key Points:

The formation of entrepreneurial teams; Characteristics of entrepreneurial companies; Employee management in entrepreneurial companies; Lean entrepreneurship; Market-oriented entrepreneurs

Case Purpose:

The entrepreneurial team plays an important role in entrepreneurial success. This case can be used to (1) evaluate and analyze the composition of the entrepreneurial team, and how to effectively achieve team complementarity; (2) make students aware of a common issue that leads to failure in entrepreneurship, namely the disconnect between entrepreneurship and the market; (3) enable students to further understand the principles of lean entrepreneurship, with a focus on grasping the essence of lean entrepreneurship.

Case Description:

Company D was founded in 2008 and its main business was assisting software developers in using cloud services to "test" their code in a more efficient manner. Wang Ming and Zhao Tao were the co-founders of Company D, having met in high school and started a web company before graduating. Company D filed for bankruptcy in 2010. In the bankruptcy declaration, Company D stated that although cloud technology tools had changed the lives of software developers, they failed to generate sufficient revenue to sustain the company's operations.

Zhao Tao believed that the failure of Company D primarily revolved around three aspects: the composition of the founding team, team communication and product development.

Regarding the founding team, both Wang Ming and Zhao Tao were engineers. While having a partner who shares a passion for the company is an advantage, neither of them had an interest in or devoted much effort to doing business. They did not consider measuring business indicators such as customer quantity or the development of distribution channels.

As for communication, Company D was founded in Beijing and supported remote work for its employees. The first critical recruitment by Company D was conducted in Shanghai, and employees did not need to come to the company's headquarters. Wang Ming and Zhao Tao believed that allowing team members to work remotely would minimize differences and make the code writing process more efficient. Unfortunately, achieving these goals turned out to be much more challenging than expected. Dealing with salaries and benefits simultaneously across different regions posed significant difficulties. Additionally, pair programming was difficult to accomplish through remote work.

Regarding product development, Zhao Tao believed that Company D should have spent more time on customer development and finding the minimum viable product (MVP). The MVP is an essential component of lean entrepreneurship and is typically tested by early users. The idea behind MVP is to avoid adding unnecessary or unwanted features to the product. However, in reality, Company D only performed minimal testing on its first product and then focused on developing new products, neglecting communication with potential users. As a result, Company D's products never truly met market demands.

In retrospect, the two founders believed that Company D should have deployed personal products more quickly and listened to customer feedback on pricing, market size, and technical challenges. They eventually realized that the market was too small and the product prices were too low to sustain the company's operations.

Questions:

1. Will having a business-oriented partner give Company D an advantage? If two business-

men start a technology-oriented company together, do you think having a business-oriented partner is still an advantage? Or should technology-oriented talents be hired?

2. Is remote work suitable for start-ups? What is your opinion?

3. Many entrepreneurs with technical background are more like engineers who enjoy inventing new things but overlook customer needs. They fail to innovate from the customer's perspective and value creation perspective. Based on this case, discuss how to address this issue.

Case Analysis:

1. When establishing an entrepreneurial team, members need to be evaluated, emphasizing both similarity and complementarity. Complementarity in knowledge and skills should be considered, while similarity in personal traits should be emphasized.

2. Although remote work is popular nowadays, it is not very suitable for startups with their unique characteristics. The organizational structure, culture, and employee relationships of startups are highly unstable, and remote work does not contribute to generating cohesion within a startup.

3. Inventors who enjoy creating new things may not necessarily be good entrepreneurs because entrepreneurs need to have a market-oriented mindset and focus on the connection between entrepreneurship and the market. Lean entrepreneurship involves using the minimum viable product, continuously testing and iterating. Through this approach, entrepreneurs can closely connect with the market, understand market dynamics, and innovate from the customer's perspective.

Case 5

Yu Minhong's Early-stage Entrepreneurial Team

Key Points:

Entrepreneurial team formation; Entrepreneurial leadership characteristics

Case Purpose:

This case aims to enable students to (1) understand the importance and uniqueness of entrepreneurial leadership, and evaluate entrepreneurial leaders; (2) think deeply about how to form entrepreneurial teams.

Case Description:

Before New Oriental was established, there were already three or four similar schools in Beijing. The main participants in New Oriental's training were students aiming to study abroad. With the increasing diversification of English requirements in work, study, and promotion, as well as the rise of studying abroad, there was a wave of English learning in China. More and more excellent teachers joined the English training industry. How could they gain a competitive advantage, expand and strengthen New Oriental? Yu Minhong believed that the English training industry must have top-notch faculty.

Training schools generally fail to grow because they excessively rely on individual lecturers. Therefore, Yu Minhong needed to find partners to help him control the quality of every aspect of English training. These individuals not only needed to have excellent professional knowledge and skills but also shared the same educational philosophy as Yu Minhong. He first thought of Wang Qiang in the United States and Xu Xiaoping in Canada. These people not only met the requirements for business expansion but, more importantly, as Yu Minhong's classmates and friends, they shared certain similarities in their thinking with him, making the cooperation more solid and long-lasting.

At this time, he met Du Zihua, who shared the same dream as him. Du Zihua had traveled to the United States, France, and Canada after graduating from graduate school. With his thorough understanding and flexible application of foreign languages, he made many friends abroad and gained numerous opportunities. However, the longer he stayed abroad and the more people he interacted with, the more he felt the importance and urgency of improving the quality of the Chinese people.

In 1994, Du Zihua, who was in training industry in Beijing, received a call from Yu Minhong. During the conversation, Yu Minhong explained New Oriental's entrepreneurship, development, his own ideals, and his desire for talent. This communication changed Du Zihua's life of individual struggle to realize his own pursuits and dreams at New Oriental.

In 1995, Yu Minhong went to Canada and invited Xu Xiaoping, a former colleague at Peking University, to join New Oriental. Subsequently, Yu Minhong went to the United States and invited Wang Qiang, who was already working at Bell Labs, to join New Oriental.

In 1997, another classmate of Yu Minhong, Bao Fanyi, rushed back from Canada to join New Oriental. New Oriental was like a magnetic field, gathering the dreams of young people and releasing the pent-up energy accumulated in them. From 1994 to 2000, Du Zihua, Xu Xiaoping, Wang Qiang, Hu Min, Bao Fanyi, He Qingquan, Qian Yongqiang, Jiang Bo, Zhou Chenggang, and others were recruited successively under Yu Minhong's leadership.

As an enterprise in the education industry, teachers constitute the core competitiveness of New Oriental. Yu Minhong, starting from student needs and upholding the innovative thinking of "doing a little more and doing it better than others," built a team reasonably, sought market gaps, and continuously improved New Oriental's business system. For example, at that time, New Oriental provided overseas consulting services, and students could obtain knowledge about basic application steps, differences in how various countries treat international students, processes for universities to award scholarships, and the differences between pursuing a master's degree and a doctorate.

In 1995, Yu Minhong realized that students' demand for English training was no longer limited to overseas examinations. Hu Min, who joined New Oriental in 1995, developed a highly popular IELTS English exam training program. Xu Xiaoping, Wang Qiang, Du Zihua, and others each contributed their abilities in areas such as overseas consulting, basic English, publishing, and online platforms, constructing a smooth product chain for New Oriental. For example, Xu Xiaoping offered visa courses, Wang Qiang provided "American Thinking" training methods, and Du Zihua offered "Film Audio-Visual Training Methods," among others.

Yu Minhong's success lies in building a young and passionate team at New Oriental. When it comes to team formation, the team in *Journey to the West* is recognized as a golden combination. The four members have different personalities but each possesses irreplaceable strengths. For example, Tang Sanzang is compassionate, has a sense of mission and organizational design ability, focuses on behavioral norms and work standards, and serves as the team's leader and core. Sun Wukong is highly skilled, quickly understands and completes tasks, and is the backbone and tough figure of the team. Although Zhu Bajie has low strength and is lazy, he is good at livening up the work atmosphere to prevent the Journey to the West from becoming too dull. Sha Wujing is diligent and down-to-earth, usually silent and unremarkable, but can remain stable and steady the situation at critical moments.

New Oriental's entrepreneurial team is somewhat similar to Tang Sanzang's team. Yu Minhong's amiability, Wang Qiang's straightforwardness, Xu Xiaoping's passion, Du Zihua's free-spiritedness, Bao Fanyi's stability—the distinct personalities of these five individuals create an atmosphere of nonconformity at New Oriental.

Yu Minhong dared to choose these people as his entrepreneurial partners, and has achieved the legend of New Oriental. In this regard, he is a successful entrepreneurial team leader. He has a clear understanding that New Oriental people are straightforward and never conceal their emotions or cater to others' ideas. They communicate directly, speak their minds, and have created a culture of combining criticism with tolerance at New Oriental. Criticism enables New Oriental people to dare to criticize each other and correct mistakes, while tolerance allows them to understand each other and continue cooperation after criticism.

Questions:

1. On the entrepreneurial path, if you could only choose two people from the four mentioned individuals in *Journey to the West* to be members of your entrepreneurial team, whom would you choose?

2. There is no doubt that Yu Minhong is a successful entrepreneurial team leader. What qualities do you think an entrepreneurial team leader should possess?

Case Analysis:

1. Entrepreneurs need to know what they possess in order to know what they need from others. To choose more adaptable collaborators, entrepreneurs must first assess themselves in terms of knowledge base, professional skills, motivation, commitment, and personality traits.

2. Entrepreneurial team leaders generally need to have qualities such as insight, effective negotiation skills, team management and building capabilities, an optimistic attitude, innovativeness, and alertness.

Case 6

Chengjiang Pharmaceuticals: How to Repair the Rift Between Founders?

Key Points:

Entrepreneurial team formation and evaluation; The characteristics of entrepreneurial ventures; Conflicts and management of an entrepreneurial team

Case Purpose:

This case aims to help students understand the conflicts and management issues within entrepreneurial teams through the changing relationship between Sun Jiaming and Zhou Yunlong, and explore the management of entrepreneurial team relationships.

Case Description:

Sun Jiaming and Zhou Yunlong were classmates in high school and college. After graduation, Zhou Yunlong entered a large state-owned pharmaceutical factory to work in quality inspection, while Sun Jiaming was assigned to a state-owned chemical factory to engage in technical research and development.

During a class reunion, they had an in-depth conversation. They both felt that it was difficult to fully utilize their talents in their current jobs. At that time, they had some savings, and the policy environment was favorable, so they decided to start a business together.

1. Development with Concerted Effort

In early 1994, both of them resigned from their jobs. In February 1994, they founded a synthetic chemical plant, with an initial registered capital of 250,000 yuan. They rented facilities and equipment from others for production. Zhou Yunlong was responsible for product sales and external contacts, while Sun Jiaming was responsible for technology, product research and development, and production.

Due to Sun Jiaming's dedication to research and strong technical development abilities, and Zhou Yunlong's good interpersonal skills and ability to make friends, the company successfully produced its first product, Shudantong rough product, in its first year, generating sales revenue of 500,000 yuan and a profit of over 1 million yuan. In 1999, the enterprise increased its registered capital to 15 million yuan and changed its name to Chengjiang Pharmaceutical and Chemical Co., Ltd., focusing on the manufacturing and export of pharmaceutical intermediates. In 2005, the company further increased its registered capital to 100 million yuan, with annual revenue of nearly 300 million yuan and a net profit of nearly 80 million yuan.

Throughout the years of cooperation, both of them consistently increased their capital contributions in the same proportion. The division of labor remained the same with Sun Jiaming focusing on internal operations and Zhou Yunlong handling external affairs. They maintained an open and trustworthy relationship with each other.

2. Breeding Cracks

As the enterprise grew, it received various honors. Sun Jiaming believed that Zhou Yunlong should not overly emphasize the importance of the sales department. In order to standardize internal management, Sun Jiaming formulated many rules and regulations. He believed that violations of the rules should be strictly enforced. However, Zhou Yunlong believed that rules and regulations were just a means of management, and special circumstances should be handled accordingly. They had several arguments because of this difference in opinion.

Since the 2008 international financial crisis, the two had different ideas about the company's future development. Sun Jiaming believed that the company should continue to adhere to its own characteristics, focus on API and moderately develop preparations, with a commitment to increasing market share in both the domestic and European/American markets. He advocated maintaining a technology-oriented approach, improving product yields, reducing production costs, enhancing product quality, and reducing overall pollution emissions through process improvement and scientific and technological development; it should take the path of specialization and concentrate on the pharmaceutical industry.

On the other hand, Zhou Yunlong believed that in order to succeed in business, the company should always stay one step ahead of others, and that competitiveness was crucial. He advocated leveraging resources through the capital market, mergers and acquisitions, and diversification to achieve leapfrog development for the company. Zhou Yunlong suggested that the company should have an open mindset and make use of the power of the capital market. He believed that making formulations and developing anti-AIDS drugs required significant investments, and the company could consider introducing venture capital and going public, even though it would dilute their shares to some extent. However, this would enhance the company's strength and reduce risks. He believed that despite the unfavorable market conditions since the international financial crisis, it was a good time for companies with aspirations for further development. With correct decision-making, adjustments in product structure, increased technological content, and the use of capital, the company should be able to maintain a 20% growth in net profit in the coming years.

3. Dilemma

The differences and conflicts between Sun Jiaming and Zhou Yunlong continued to escalate. Zhou Yunlong proposed that one person should take full responsibility for the company's operations, and that person must achieve a 20% growth rate in net profit for the next three years. If they failed to meet the target, they would have to transfer shares to compensate for the performance gap and relinquish their management rights. Zhou Yunlong also promised that Sun Jiaming could make the choice first.

Sun Jiaming believed that if he took on the responsibility, although he would gain the authority to manage the company and a sense of achievement if the target was reached, he would also have to bear the risk of transferring shares. If Zhou Yunlong took the responsibility, and he successfully achieved the target, Sun Jiaming would lose the authority to manage the company. If Zhou Yunlong failed, although Sun Jiaming could increase his shares and gain management rights, there would still be a risk of jeopardizing the company. Therefore, regardless of who took the responsibility, the risk was significant.

Questions:

1. Why did Sun Jiaming and Zhou Yunlong choose to start a business together instead of pursuing individual ventures?

2. Why was Chengjiang Pharmaceuticals able to achieve good performance in the first decade? What caused the conflicts between Sun Jiaming and Zhou Yunlong afterwards?

3. If you were Sun Jiaming, would you choose to continue with equal division of work or to authorize one person to take full responsibility? If you choose to continue with division of work, how would you handle the situation?

Case Analysis:

1. Entrepreneurship often takes the form of teamwork, and a strong entrepreneurial team is an effective guarantee for entrepreneurial success. By forming a team, entrepreneurs not only supplement each other's resources but also mitigate risks. More importantly, the cooperation and encouragement among team members can alleviate the psychological burden on entrepreneurs and motivate their growth.

2. During the early stages of entrepreneurship, entrepreneurial teams often collaborate effectively. As the entrepreneurial venture grows, management becomes more complex, and issues such as power and profit distribution become focal points of contention. As the saying goes, "It's easy to share hardships, but hard to share wealth."

3. Multiple leaders often lead to management confusion and unclear responsibilities, so

division of labor must be clearly defined. Managing an entrepreneurial team is highly complex, and various conflicts often arise, especially when founders fail to communicate effectively and mishandle their relationships, resulting in various contradictions.

Case 7

Zhang Chaoyang's Early Entrepreneurial Journey

Key Points:

The roles of entrepreneur and external environment in opportunity identification

Case Purpose:

This case aims to analyze the factors that influence entrepreneurial opportunity identification, with a focus on the following aspects: (1) the role of entrepreneurs in recognizing entrepreneurial opportunities, examining their alertness, personal traits, and cognitive learning abilities; (2) the impact of the external environment on entrepreneurial opportunity identification, such as the impact of financing and market conditions.

Case Description:

Zhang Chaoyang was born in Xi'an, Shaanxi Province in 1964. He graduated from the Department of Physics at Tsinghua University in 1986. In the same year, he received the Li Zhengdao Scholarship and went to the United States for further study. In 1993, he obtained his doctoral degree from the Massachusetts Institute of Technology (MIT). In 1994, he served as the Asia-Pacific Regional Liaison Officer for MIT. In 1995, he became the Chief Representative of the United States-based company, Internet Solutions International (ISI), in China. In 1996, he founded the company Aitexin. In 1998, Aitexin officially launched its product, Sohu, and changed its name to Sohu. In 2000, Sohu went public in the United States.

Zhang Chaoyang's entrepreneurial spirit was shaped by the regional culture of Xi'an, the campus culture of Tsinghua University, and the Western modern culture of the United States. He possessed both a reserved and pragmatic nature, as well as a trendy, avant-garde, and fashionable side.

In July 1995, the Silicon Valley-style entrepreneurship in the United States sparked Zhang Chaoyang's enthusiasm for entrepreneurship. He realized the incredible commercial and social value of the Internet economy and decided to return to China to start his own business. Zhang Chaoyang approached ISI with the idea of establishing China Online, and the president of ISI shared a similar vision, leading to their agreement. In 1995, Zhang Chaoyang served as the Chief Representative of ISI in China, using the Internet to collect and disseminate economic information.

His experience at ISI made Zhang Chaoyang realize the enormous potential of the Chinese Internet market. In February 1998, Zhang Chaoyang launched Sohu, the first fully Chinese online search engine. In March 1998, he secured a total investment of 2.1 million USD from companies including Intel, marking a turning point for his career. In September 1998, Sohu established its Shanghai branch, and in June 1999, the Guangzhou branch began to be established. In 2000, Sohu successfully went public in the United States and acquired the ChinaRen community website. The rapid development of online communities added a new dimension to portal websites, making Sohu one of the largest portal websites in China and laying the foundation for its rapid business expansion.

Subsequently, Zhang Chaoyang recognized the potential benefits that short message services could bring to the Internet and attempted to operate it as an industry closely integrated with the Internet. In 2001, Zhang Chaoyang invested millions to create the "Sohu Mobile Fashion Tour" and served as the Chief Image Spokesperson, achieving great success.

On July 17, 2002, Sohu became profitable. On February 25, 2003, Sohu launched the game *Knight* and announced its entry into the online game market. Zhang Chaoyang was awarded second place on the "2003 List of Wealthiest Chinese Technology Entrepreneurs of Listed Companies," and he ranked in the top three on "Top 50 IT Magnates in China in 2003."

From 1999 to 2001, while the Chinese Internet market was booming, Sohu remained stagnant, and its board of directors encountered problems. In March-April 2001, Sohu's stock fell below 1 USD, risking delisting from NASDAQ. The situation was extremely challenging, but Zhang Chaoyang successfully refined himself in the face of adversity. From 2001 to 2004, he addressed the problems and ultimately pulled Sohu out of its predicament.

Zhang Chaoyang believed that the reason Sohu overcame its difficulties and continued to experience rapid growth was that both he and Sohu's management had strong reflective abilities. It was this ability to reflect that led Zhang Chaoyang and Sohu's management to recognize that Sohu excelled in marketing but fell short in product development. Zhang Chaoyang believed that everyone had their own unique growth experiences, which would inevitably lead to biases in perception. Only by constantly adjusting oneself, approaching everything with respect, and maintaining composure in the face of both praise and adversity can one break through and achieve success.

Questions:

1. Based on this case, analyze the role of the entrepreneur in opportunity identification.

2. Analyze the role of external environment in opportunity identification.

Case Analysis:

1. The characteristics, experiences, cognition, social network relationships, and creativity of entrepreneurs can all influence the identification of entrepreneurial opportunities. This question can be analyzed from the perspectives of Zhang Chaoyang's alertness, personal traits, and cognitive learning abilities.

2. In addition to individual factors, the external environment also plays a crucial role

in opportunity identification. The process of opportunity identification is the result of interaction between entrepreneurs and the environment. Entrepreneurs use various channels and methods to grasp and obtain information about environmental changes, thereby discovering gaps or deficiencies in products, services, raw materials, and organizational methods in the real world. They find possibilities for improving or creating "means-ends" relationships and ultimately identify entrepreneurial opportunities that may bring new products, services, raw materials, and organizational methods. This question can be analyzed from the perspective of the influence of financing and market conditions on opportunity identification.

Case 8

The Failure of Company E

Key Points:

Market orientation; Team building; Entrepreneurial marketing

Case Purpose:

The purpose of this case is to help students (1) realize a serious problem that that often arises in the entrepreneurial process—neglecting customers and the market; (2) understand the complexity of new business creation and the importance of legitimacy to start-ups.

Case Description:

In 2009, Wang Ming discovered that storing and organizing photos was a difficult task. When he discussed this issue with engineer Zhang Qiang, he found that Zhang Qiang also faced challenges in dealing with photos. Moreover, the more photos they took, the less likely they were to review them.

At that time, there was no product on the market that provided photo storage and organization while encouraging people to regularly review their photos to some extent. So the two of them decided to start a business and create a model that offered photo storage and sorting services. In June 2011, they met Fan Hua and developed him into a partner. Fan Hua had previously worked in interactive and visual design at a company in Shanghai. The three of them spent several months designing the service model, which they named EP. EP accurately discovered photos on computer desktops, allowed users to upload photos through web services, and then organized and tagged the best ones, providing convenience, speed, and user-friendliness.

Wang Ming and Zhang Qiang invested 1.8 million US dollars raised from angel investors into product development. In March 2013, they launched EP1.0. Through the App connected to EP, users could see all their past photos, and for a certain fee, they could store a large number of photos. EP also had a great feature called "Flashback," which sent users an email every day with photos they had taken on the same day in the past. The service of EP was highly praised, and the App had over 1,000 user reviews with a rating of 4.5 stars. However, in the summer of 2013, EP suddenly ceased operations.

In general, EP's failure was due to its founders spending too much time and effort perfecting their service. EP's subscribers couldn't easily share photos with their friends, thus encouraging them to become EP users, as the service did not have viral dissemination. The EP team realized this problem and attempted various methods to speed up service dissemination, but they were unsuccessful. Additionally, EP did not invest anything in advertising and marketing; they put all their funds into the research and improvement of their service and product. As a result, while other apps were attracting numerous users, EP had less than 19,000 registered users.

In the weeks leading up to bankruptcy, EP's founders attempted to raise more funds. However, with the proliferation of other similar Apps, users could easily switch to those photo-processing Apps. Furthermore, while EP's business model relied on paid subscriptions, many of EP's competitors' services were already free. As a result, investors turned them down. They also submitted proposals to potential acquirers, but they all failed. In the end, EP had to cease operations due to running out of funds.

Questions:

1. If you were planning to create a company to solve a certain problem, list three key points you learned from the case that you should avoid in the future.

2. What is the difference between pursuing opportunities to solve problems and creating an enterprise? What mistakes has EP made in this regard?

Case Analysis:

1. Entrepreneurship needs to be market-oriented. Neglecting market orientation and customer needs will inevitably lead to failure in entrepreneurship. From team formation and company establishment to entrepreneurial marketing and resource integration, all are important parts that cannot be ignored. Neglecting market orientation, neglecting company establishment, lacking necessary entrepreneurial marketing strategies, and ignoring innovation in subsequent business models are the reasons for EP's failure.

2. Pursuing an opportunity to solve a problem is relatively simple, but creating a company becomes complex. Business management involves various and complex activities. Moreover, creating a company is easier when it is opportunity-oriented.

Case 9

A Practical "Fix"

Key Points:

Resource bricolage; Types of resource bricolage

Case Purpose:

Through two micro-cases, students are guided to understand what resource bricolage is, the general types of resource bricolage, and their advantages and disadvantages.

Case Description:

Bi Kegui Selling Octopuses

In 2004, Bi Kegui took over the business founded by his parents. The enterprise was mainly engaged in exporting processed fish, shellfish, and shrimp products, with annual sales of over 20 million yuan. As the cost of raw materials and production continued to rise, the company's profits became increasingly low. Bi Kegui decided to advertise for investment opportunities.

In 2006, a representative from a Japanese company, Yu Yang, approached Bi Kegui, hoping to sign a $500,000 contract at a price of $6,000 per ton of finished octopus. This was because Bi Kegui had an idle production line in a separate workshop that met the Japanese company's production requirements. The local octopus in Dalian was not the variety the client needed, so Bi Kegui purchased 150 tons of octopus from Fujian and processed it according to the client's requirements. This business deal earned Bi Kegui over $40,000. More importantly, there were monthly orders worth $200,000. While continuing normal production of other seafood products, the company's output doubled.

The exported products to Japan were octopus heads and tentacles, and the remaining necks and tips of tentacles became surplus products that piled up in the warehouse. In April 2007, while shopping, Bi Kegui discovered someone selling octopus balls made from squid tentacles. The seller explained that they used squid as a substitute because it was difficult to find octopus as raw material. Bi Kegui sold the surplus products to the seller, earning an additional 200,000 yuan in profit for the factory each year. At the same time, Bi Kegui realized that a box of octopus balls sold for 3 yuan, while the cost was less than 30 cents, which greatly inspired him. In the traditional concept, export processing companies generally focus on cost control and rarely consider market and sales issues. Bi Kegui wanted to break away from the business model of merely processing products for processing fees and be able to directly sell their own products.

During the Spring Festival of 2008, in response to the needs of citizens during the Spring Festival, Bi Kegui packaged fish and shrimp products into gift boxes for sale. While promoting the gift boxes, Bi Kegui met Wang Zhendong, a sea cucumber dealer in Dalian. After negotiation, Bi Kegui agreed to share 40% of the sales profit with Wang Zhendong and allowed him to sell the seafood snack products in his sea cucumber specialty store. Wang Zhendong sold sea cucumbers and abalone, while Bi Kegui sold seafood snack products, complementing each other. In less than a month, the sales of seafood snack products exceeded 100,000 yuan.

The Early Entrepreneurial Journey of Thunder

In 2002, Thunder's founders Cheng Hao and Zou Shenglong started a business together, but the company soon encountered difficulties. They decided to discuss a transformation. Cheng Hao found that among the five major Internet applications - portals, email, search, instant messaging, and downloads - only downloads did not have a mainstream provider. However, for large files such as movies and online games, users had to download them to use them. Cheng Hao and Zou Shenglong decided to develop Thunder. Thunder used grid-based multi-resource threading technology, which provided extremely fast download speeds. To release the product as quickly as possible, Cheng Hao focused on addressing the most important concerns of the target consumers during the development process, abandoning research on other product details. Although early versions had many flaws, Thunder gained a competitive advantage in the market due to its speed.

In 2004, Cheng Hao approached Lei Jun, the president of Kingsoft, who gave him a chance to test the product. The test showed that Thunder's download speed was 20 times faster than other tools. As a result, Kingsoft agreed to recommend its game users to use Thunder's client software for free downloads of their popular games. After gaining recognition from Kingsoft, Thunder quickly reached agreements with other online game manufacturers. Within two months, Thunder's daily new user count increased from less than 300 to over 10,000. In six months, Thunder had 3 million users, with 95% of them brought in by their online game partners. With a considerable user base, Thunder quickly achieved a balanced budget through advertising, software bundling, wireless services, and pay-per-performance bid ranking ads. Thunder then continuously released upgraded versions to fix software vulnerabilities.

Questions:

1. What is resource bricolage strategy? How did Bi Kegui implement the resource bricolage strategy?

2. What type of resource bricolage strategy did Thunder adopt and why?

Case Analysis:

1. Resource bricolage includes three key elements: utilizing existing resources, integrating resources for new purposes, and making do with what is available. Bi Kegui continuously used various resources at hand to find new opportunities, such as breaking habitual ways of thinking, reusing available resources, making do with what was available, and integrating resources.

2. Generally, resource bricolage strategy can be divided into comprehensive bricolage and selective bricolage. Comprehensive bricolage refers to entrepreneurs using bricolage methods in terms of material resources, human resources, technical resources, institutional norms, and customer markets for an extended period, even after the company's cash flow has stabilized. This behavior makes it difficult for companies to form standardized rules and regulations for internal management and also faces resistance in the external market due to the use of low-standard resources. Selective bricolage refers to entrepreneurs having some selectivity in their bricolage process. They tend to only choose one or two areas for bricolage to avoid the self-reinforcing cycle of comprehensive bricolage. They only use bricolage when resources are scarce in the early stages of entrepreneurship. Thunder adopted selective bricolage in early product development and, after gaining market recognition, shifted to product optimization (resource optimization) rather than selective bricolage.

Case 10

The Entrepreneurial Journey of Langming Technology in AI

Key Points:

The Timmons' Model of Entrepreneurial Process; Entrepreneurial opportunity; Entrepreneurial resources; Entrepreneurship

Case Purpose:

Through this case, students will gain an in-depth understanding of the application of The Timmons Model of Entrepreneurial Process in entrepreneurship, the recognition of opportunities and utilization of resources by entrepreneurs at different stages of entrepreneurship, and the entrepreneurial spirit demonstrated by Guo Ming, the founder of Langming Technology, in the company's different stages of development.

Case Description:

1. Initial Stage of Entrepreneurship

In July 2009, the 21-year-old Guo Ming graduated from Tsinghua University's Computer Science Experiment Class, also known as the Yao Class, which was founded by Academician Andrew Chi-Chih Yao. By the time he graduated, Guo Ming had already spent two years as an intern at Microsoft Research Asia, Beijing, where he was involved in the development of a face recognition project in computer vision. During this period, Guo Ming was exposed to and involved in many cutting-edge projects in the industry, and his intuition told him that computer vision technology had great potential in the future.

Upon graduation, Guo Ming shared his intuition and ideas with his classmate, Tang Xia, who was also an intern at Microsoft, and they decided to start a business together two years later. Guo Ming believed that hardware and software are the two wings of artificial intelligence, but they only had software technology and little knowledge of related hardware.

Therefore, he planned to go to Stanford University in the United States to study 3D camera hardware knowledge and then return to China to start a business. At that time, e-commerce, group buying, and games were popular in China, and artificial intelligence was not yet well known to the public. Tang Xia, who was then a coach of the training team for the Olympiad in Informatics in China, recommended Zhang Bin, a younger student from the Yao Class, to Guo Ming. This formed the embryonic form of the three-person entrepreneurial team.

In 2010, the three of them participated in the national Challenge Cup competition and won the championship with a game called "Crows Coming" based on face recognition and face tracking technology. The game attracted the attention of Legend Star, which was so optimistic about the market value of the technology that it decided to make an angel investment, hoping the three would continue to launch and commercialize other products. At the same time, they were invited to join Legend Star's CEO Training Program to learn about entrepreneurial management practices.

Since their contact with Legend Star, Guo Ming had the idea of starting a company. In 2011, Langming Technology Co., Ltd. (hereinafter referred to as Langming Technology) was incorporated in Beijing with Guo Ming as CEO. However, Guo Ming's plan to study abroad did not change because he always believed that artificial intelligence technology needed a combination of software and hardware. Shortly after Langming Technology was founded, Guo Ming started his studies in the US, while Tang Xia and Zhang Bin attended Legend Star's CEO Training Program. Langming Technology was temporarily operating as a game developer, and the company's affairs were handled by the three via video conference. Their entrepreneurial story aroused a sensation in the Yao Class, and dozens of younger students from the Yao Class came to intern at the recently established Langming Technology.

2. Start-up Stage of Entrepreneurship

Deep down, Guo Ming did not believe that games were their direction of development, as they were not passionate about games. One day, Guo Ming came across a news article that said, "Facebook acquires an Israeli face recognition company that has been established for less than a year for up to $100 million." This news shocked Guo Ming, and he immediately told Tang Xia and Zhang Bin about it, suggesting that they suspend game development and focus on the research and development of face recognition technology. However, the other two did not agree.

To convince them, Guo Ming conducted extensive research and consulted Prof. Andrew Chi-Chih Yao. At the same time, he learned from his teachers and classmates in the United States that not only Facebook but also Google was investing in face recognition. In the end, he concluded that image recognition technology in the field of artificial intelligence is a representative application, and face recognition may be the best way to measure this technology. Based on this, Langming Technology's development strategy gradually became clear: focusing on the development of computer vision technology, the company's first step was face recognition, the second step was object recognition, and the third step was to achieve a "machine's eye" that provides a what-you-see-is-what-you-get experience. With these materials and a clear company strategy, Tang Xia and Zhang Bin finally agreed to Guo Ming's proposal.

In August 2012, Langming Technology completed an angel investment from Legend Star and Lenovo Capital. They then fully engaged in the research and development of face recognition technology. In October of the same year, Langming Technology officially launched the cloud-based computer vision open platform called Face++, which, in an environment where artificial intelligence was not yet popular, provided a comprehensive set of world-leading visual technology services for face detection, face recognition, and facial analysis. Shortly after the launch of the Face++ platform, they began cooperation with clients such as Meitu, Jiayuan.com.

Although the face recognition technology had achieved phased results, Guo Ming knew very well that as a technology service company, technology was the core competitive advantage. Therefore, he proposed the establishment of a research institute within the company to specialize in continuous iterative research and development of technology. This idea was opposed by the other two, as they believed that the Face++ platform had just been launched and lacked a clear business model, so they should not divert their focus and resources to unrestrained technology development. In May 2013, Guo Ming dropped out of school and returned to China to set up Langming Institute. He had intended to invite his former teacher, Sun Yang, who he had interned with at Microsoft, to join, but he was politely declined. Instead, Sun Yang told Guo Ming that Li KaiFu, CEO of Sinovation Ventures, was interested in investing in Face++. Thus, in July 2013, Langming Technology closed a Series A round of funding with Sinovation Ventures.

Langming Technology focused on the cultivation of internal talents. At this point, Tang Xia's experience as a coach of the training team for the Olympiad in Informatics in China played a significant role. The first group of researchers and engineers at Langming Institute were all medalists in the Olympiad in informatics. In addition, Langming Technology has created an environment of "technological faith" that has attracted many students from Tsinghua University, Peking University, and Beihang University for internships. Many of them naturally stayed at the end of their internships.

In October 2013, Brain++, an artificial intelligence algorithm engine, was developed at Langming Institute. Based on Brain++, Langming Technology built a continuously improving and increasingly automated algorithm production line. At the same time, Brain++ could be customized to meet the fragmented demands in different vertical fields with enriched and growing algorithm combinations.

3. Entrepreneurial Development Stage

In 2014, Langming Technology started its collaboration with Ant Financial Services Group, and on March 16, 2015, at the CeBIT IT Exhibition in Hanover, Germany, Ma Yun demonstrated the face recognition payment technology of Ant Financial, which was powered by Langming Technology's face recognition technology. In the same year,

Langming Technology closed a Series B round of funding with Sinovation Ventures and Qiming Venture Partners.

Since its face recognition technology empowered Ant Financial, Langming Technology established a firm foothold in the B-end market, which made Guo Ming realize the great significance of artificial intelligence technology empowering traditional industries. As a result, Guo Ming and the other two co-founders decided to shift their business focus to the B-end market and decisively abandoned their successful C-end products, such as hot games and apps.

For the B-end market, Langming Technology first chose to open up the market from the financial sector based on their accumulated experience, and launched FaceID, a financial-grade authentication solution, which provides online authentication services for remote real-name scenarios and has been adopted by key financial institutions such as PingAn Bank, CITIC Bank and Bank of Jiangsu. In October 2015, Langming Technology launched the world's first smart camera, which became the hardware carrier for the upcoming security sector. Langming Technology has been providing urban management solutions since December 2015, when it delivered security support for the World Internet Conference in Wuzhen. Subsequently, Langming Technology has participated in the security work for the 2016 G20 Summit in Hangzhou and the 2017 BRICS Summit in Xiamen. In addition, in collaboration with the public security department, Langming Technology has built an identification photo database for "wanted" personnel, relying on real-time comparison with surveillance cameras in public places.

While the company continued to grow, organizational and management issues emerged at Langming Technology. In response, Guo Ming went to study organizational and business management.

After expanding into the finance and security sectors, in 2016, Langming Technology became a leading company in China's computer vision field. At this time, Sun Yang, Guo

Ming's former teacher during his internship at Microsoft, joined Langming Technology as the Director of Langming Institute and Chief Scientist of Langming Technology. Subsequently, Langming Institute USA, Langming Institute Nanjing, and Langming Institute Shanghai were established, each with key leaders recruited by Sun Yang. Among them, Sun Yang invited Li Lin, former chief scientist of Adobe, to be the head of Lamming Institute USA.

Guo Ming believed that the combination of industry, academia, and research was a tool to evaluate the value of current artificial intelligence innovation. Therefore, Langming Technology needed to establish an academic committee. To this end, Guo Ming invited Prof. Andrew Chi-Chih Yao to be the chief advisor of the academic committee.

By chance, Tang Xia discovered that in a 20,000-square-meter warehouse at Tmall Supermarket in Nanjing, the pickers had to walk about 40 kilometers every day. This prompted Tang Xia to consider the possibility of using intelligent means to improve warehouse logistics efficiency. In April 2018, Langming Technology acquired a robotics company and focused on the research of machine vision and intelligent scheduling algorithm technology for deep learning. In January 2019, Langming Technology's technical team led the industry by developing and releasing the world's first AIoT operating system for logistics and manufacturing. Langming Technology's self-developed artificial intelligence technology could digitally link robots with warehousing operations, achieving intelligent handling, picking, and more. This technology has been adopted by Tmall Supermarket, Procter & Gamble, and others.

Questions:

1. What are the factors that influence entrepreneurial success? What are the reasons for the mixed feelings of Langming Technology during the entrepreneurial enlightenment and early stages, and the smooth development of business during the entrepreneurial growth stage?

2. In the three stages of entrepreneurship, what entrepreneurial opportunities did Guo Ming identify? How did he accurately identify them?

3. What advantageous resources did Guo Ming utilize during the entrepreneurial process?

4. Which qualities exhibited by Guo Ming are closely related to his success? What entrepreneurial spirit did Guo Ming demonstrate during the entrepreneurial process?

Case Analysis:

1. The Timmons Model of Entrepreneurial Process suggests that successful entrepreneurial activities require an appropriate match between opportunity, team and resources and these three factors should be dynamically balanced as the entrepreneurial process evolves. The entrepreneurial process begins with opportunity identification and selection as the key focus in the early stages of entrepreneurship. In the early startup stage, the emphasis is on building the entrepreneurial team, and after the new venture is launched, the need for increased resources arises. Therefore, we can analyze the case using the Timmons Model of Entrepreneurial Process. During the entrepreneurial enlightenment period, Langming Technology had numerous opportunities but a vague positioning, relatively abundant human and technical resources, and a lack of team validation. The model's focus shifted towards the right, ultimately resulting in slow development during the entrepreneurial enlightenment period. In the early startup stage, the entrepreneurial opportunities and direction were already clear, but various external resources were abundant yet difficult to obtain, resulting in an imbalanced state with the model's focus shifted towards the left. During the entrepreneurial growth stage, Langming Technology achieved a relative balance in terms of opportunities, team, and resources, enabling the smooth development of the company's new business.

2. Prior experience, cognitive factors, social network connections, and entrepreneurial alertness are key factors influencing opportunity identification. In the initial period of

entrepreneurship, Guo Ming's internship at Microsoft Research Asia, Beijing made him realize the importance of computer vision technology, leading him to share this insight with his classmate Tang Xia, and they decided to start a business. In the early startup stage, when Facebook acquired an Israeli facial recognition company less than a year old for a staggering $100 million, Guo Ming recognized the development trend of facial recognition technology. As a result, he collected information, and the development strategy and direction of Langming Technology became clear. During the entrepreneurial growth stage, Langming timely shifted its focus from the C-end to the B-end market, which was another successful identification of entrepreneurial opportunities by Guo Ming.

3. Entrepreneurial resources refer to the specific assets that a start-up requires in the process of creating value. These resources can be tangible or intangible in form and are essential conditions for the establishment and operation of new ventures. During the initial stage, the resources manifested in opportunities such as the Microsoft internship, the Challenge Cup competition, investment from Legend Star, and the support of younger students from the Yao Class. In the early startup stage, the resources manifested in the support of Li Kaifu, as well as the participation of students from Tsinghua University, Peking University, and Beihang University. During the entrepreneurial development stage, the resources manifested in the collaboration with Ant Financial Services Group, continuous financing, and the addition of talents like Sun Yang and Li Lin.

4. Entrepreneurial traits typically encompass four dimensions: achievement motivation, internal locus of control, risk preference, and innovation ability. Entrepreneurship refers to the comprehensive abilities of entrepreneurs to establish and manage businesses. It is an important and distinctive intangible production factor that represents the unique personal qualities, values, and thinking patterns of entrepreneurs. Specifically, entrepreneurship includes innovative spirit, adventurous spirit, entrepreneurial spirit, and tolerant spirit.

Case 11

Dingdong's Business Model

Key Points:

PEST analysis; Business model elements

Case Purpose:

Through this case study, students will become familiar with how companies design their business models based on market conditions. They will understand the factors that influence the content of business models in the new retail environment and master the general logic process of the canvas design of a business model.

Case Description:

1. Rising with the Trend

In May 2017, Liang Changlin, a retired soldier, founded Dingdong (Cayman) Limited, which is dedicated to solving the problem of difficult grocery shopping for users. Over the course of four years, Dingdong started in Shanghai, expanded to most areas in the Yangtze River Delta, and further developed in Beijing, Guangzhou, Shenzhen, Chengdu, Dongguan, Foshan, etc. It focused on providing users with a fresh food consumption experience that guarantees quality, delivery time within 29 minutes, and a specified product range through a service model combining direct sourcing from origin, pre-positioned warehouses for distribution, and technology-driven industry chain upgrades. It has become a trusted Internet company for users' livelihoods.

In the fresh food e-commerce market, there are Freshippo, Missfresh, Duoduo Food, etc., with various operating models. For example, the "independent store+self-pickup" community e-commerce model of Freshippo, Meituan Preferred, and community group purchase model of Duoduo Food based on "group leaders + self-pickup". In the challenging early stages of entrepreneurship, Dingdong grew stronger. Through research, site selection, equipment installation, and product categorization, Dingdong finally found a successful path to avoid homogeneous competition and achieve differentiated development—the pre-positioned warehouse model.

As an early beneficiary of the Internet economy, the logistics industry has naturally entered a new era of rapid development. In 2016, the *Implementation Plan for Creating a Good Market Environment to Promote the Integrated Development of Transport and Logistics* formulated by the National Development and Reform Commission proposed that by 2020, a group of transport and logistics enterprises with strong competitiveness should be formed, and the cold chain transport service specifications should be improved to realize end-to-end uninterrupted cold chain logistics. From the origin to the dining table, the delivery time for goods became increasingly shorter, bringing more possibilities to the development of the fresh food e-commerce industry in China.

In recent years, the state has issued several policies to encourage the development of agricultural e-commerce, creating significant opportunities in the fresh food market. In 2019, the *Notice on Promoting the Interconnection of Agriculture and Commerce to Improve the Supply Chain of Agricultural Products* was released, which proposed strengthening post-production commercialization facilities and cold chain logistics facilities. Central financial funds supported these two types of projects with a funding proportion of no less than 70%.

In the Internet era, the continuous shift in consumer attitudes towards consumption has driven the continuous development of the fresh food e-commerce industry, bringing market opportunities to Dingdong. At the same time, many phenomena unfavorable to the food delivery industry have emerged. For example, the rise of the "health-conscious" trend has led some health-conscious individuals to start cooking for themselves. Additionally, the fresh food industry is experiencing a transformation in terms of industry scale and technological environment. Firstly, there is the rural land transfer and the industrialization of agriculture. Secondly, the expansion of new retail companies like Dingdong is driving upstream companies to improve their quality and services. Thirdly, technologies such as logistics, big data, and artificial intelligence are rapidly developing in China, leading to rapid optimization of the industry's value chain's intermediate links.

2. The Secret to Success

(1) A strong foundation

Dingdong's increasing market share is closely related to its own strong capabilities and foundation. Stable fresh agricultural product suppliers, pre-positioned warehouse distribution with 29-minute delivery, powerful big data analytics capabilities, expanding market scale, substantial capital investments, high repurchase rates, and service levels have contributed to the significant development of Dingdong.

Stable fresh agricultural product suppliers: Dingdong's procurement model mainly relies on "city wholesale purchase + direct supply from brand merchants." For perishable fresh products such as vegetables and seafood that are difficult to transport over long distances, Dingdong mainly adopts a "city wholesale purchase" model to ensure product freshness and reduce losses. Under this model, replenishing inventory is easier, the product range is relatively complete, and prices are relatively stable. For meat products, they are directly supplied by brand merchants to ensure product safety and quality.

Pre-positioned warehouse with 29-minute delivery: Dingdong adopts a distributed warehousing model rather than a centralized warehousing model, which lays the foundation for its efficient delivery. The "29-minute delivery + 0 delivery fee + 0 minimum order" service better meets the needs of immediate consumption. In terms of delivery, Dingdong has years of service experience, a highly stable delivery team, and a self-developed intelligent scheduling and last-mile delivery system, which lays the foundation for its high-efficiency delivery service.

Powerful big data analytics capabilities: Dingdong integrates big data throughout the entire supply chain to enhance user experience through technologies such as order forecasting, user profiling, intelligent recommendations, intelligent scheduling, route optimization, and self-service customer support. According to data, Dingdong's big data analysis keeps its average daily unsold loss rate below 3% and logistics loss rate at only 0.3%.

Expanding market scale: Dingdong has made deep inroads in the Yangtze River Delta market. During the 2019 Spring Festival, Dingdong announced its entry into Hangzhou, followed by entering cities such as Suzhou, Ningbo, and Wuxi. Although Dingdong entered multiple cities in the Yangtze River Delta, Shanghai remains its center of focus, with a dense network within a 200-kilometer radius of Shanghai. This also means that from the perspective of the supply chain, it is possible for Dingdong in different cities to share resources in the supply chain. In August 2019, Dingdong officially entered Shenzhen. Before entering Shenzhen, the Dingdong team completed the preparatory work, including user research, supply chain backend construction, establishment of central and pre-positioned warehouses, and frontline staff configuration, in just 46 days.

Substantial capital investments: As a rising star in the fresh food e-commerce industry, Dingdong has been favored by capital investors. It has completed multiple rounds of financing, with investment from top institutions such as Capital Today and Sequoia Capital. In 2018 alone, Dingdong completed five rounds of financing.

High repurchase rates and service levels: Dingdong particularly values long-term user retention and adopts a strategy of "repurchase rate is king." Data shows that Dingdong's long-term retention rate reached 38% in the 31st month, and the average monthly consumption for old users is 6.5 times, leading the industry. The "Recipe Recommendations" feature in the Dingdong app also increases user engagement. When users click on a product, the recipe and corresponding purchase links for ingredients and seasonings are displayed below the product details, making it convenient for users to purchase all the ingredients in one place.

Focusing on "selling vegetables" with lower average order value: Fresh food accounts for 75%~80% of the product structure of Dingdong. To reduce the purchasing threshold for users, Dingdong introduced a "0 yuan minimum order + 0 yuan delivery fee" policy when entering new cities. As a result, the average order value is relatively low. Data shows that in 2017, the average order value for Dingdong was around 30-40 yuan; in 2018, it reached around 50 yuan; and in 2019, Dingdong tested a 5 yuan delivery fee for orders below 28 yuan in certain areas of Shanghai, resulting in an increase in the average order value to 60 yuan.

(2) Seeking external support

The successful development of Dingdong's business relies on every link in the supply chain. Dingdong actively cooperates with various partners to pursue win-win cooperation.

Dingdong has signed a strategic cooperation agreement with Shanghai Farm, and appointed it as the "Dingdong Cooperation Base." They work together to promote the transformation and upgrading of Shanghai's agricultural product production and sales integration and promote the integration of online and offline fresh retail models. At the same time, Dingdong collaborates with over 200 cooperatives and over 3,000 farmers to achieve direct sourcing from the source. Direct sourcing reduces the involvement of intermediaries, minimizes losses, maintains product freshness, and reduces costs.

In 2019, at the local fresh food partner conference of Ali, Dingdong and the public praise "Eleme" signed a strategic cooperation agreement to explore various cooperative directions, including logistics, marketing, after-sales service, and membership. Dingdong has become an important member of Ali's local life ecosystem partnership.

Dingdong has always used the pre-positioned warehouse model to provide "grocery shopping at home" services. To shorten the last mile of delivery, Dingdong sets up pre-positioned warehouses in various community locations, ensuring a high-density small-scale warehousing model. Therefore, the warehouse leasing party becomes a vital partner for

Dingdong. Establishing friendly cooperation with the lessors to obtain premium warehouse locations has always been a focus for Dingdong.

(3) Clear target customers

Dingdong's target customers can be divided into the following four categories.

Catering enterprises. Dingdong has established strategic partnerships with catering enterprises in terms of manpower, ingredients, and supply chain, delivering high-quality fresh food to them.

Fast paced office workers. In today's fast-paced life, many office workers struggle to find time to cook a meal for themselves. Going to a reliable market, choosing groceries, and going back home to cook all require a significant amount of time. Dingdong's doorstep delivery service is tailored for office workers who are busy during weekdays and prefer to stay at home on weekends.

Elderly people with limited mobility. Many elderly people face difficulties in going to distant markets if they have limited mobility. Dingdong's doorstep delivery service not only fulfills their desire to cook for themselves but also avoids the physical burden of traveling.

Leasing enterprises. Dingdong temporarily leases the idle cold storage to other enterprises or individuals.

(4) Diverse marketing models and multiple revenue sources

Dingdong's marketing models include the following: ①reward programs for bringing in new users; ②green card membership system; ③big data prediction and intelligent recommendation.

The main sources of Dingdong's revenue include sales revenue from providing fresh products such as vegetables, fruits, and seafood, platform service commissions, in-app advertising revenue, annual membership fees of 88 yuan per person for the green card membership, cold storage leasing revenue, and ancillary services revenue from warehousing and logistics platforms. The cost structure of Dingdong includes costs for fresh procurement, storage and cold chain delivery, labor costs, construction and rental costs of pre-positioned warehouses, lightweight marketing and promotion expenses, app development and big data algorithm costs, as well as website operation and maintenance costs.

Questions:

1. How is Dingdong's current environment? Analyze using PEST.

2. Based on the business model canvas, please analyze the business model of Dingdong.

3. How does Dingdong identify and attract its target users? What are the characteristics of these users?

Case Analysis:

1. PEST analysis refers to the analysis of the macro environment for the survival and development of enterprises. P refers to politics, E refers to economy, S refers to society, and T refers to technology. Economic factors mainly include economic development level, scale, growth rate, government revenue and expenditure, inflation rate, etc; Political elements mainly include political system, government policy, national industrial policy, relevant laws and regulations, etc; Social elements mainly include population, values, moral standards, etc; The technological elements include breakthroughs in high-tech, process technology and basic research.

2. The business model is the core logic through which a company creates value. The logical aspects of a business model are mainly reflected in the following areas. ①Value discovery. Clarify the source of value creation, as a company's profitability depends on

whether it has customers. ②Value matching. Identify partners and realize value creation. ③Value acquisition. Formulate competitive strategies to capture innovative value. Key elements of a business model include customer segmentation, value proposition, channel, customer relationship, revenue source, core resources, key businesses, important partners, and cost structure.

3. The target user group is the user group targeted by the company. These groups share certain characteristics that enable companies to create value. This question is divided into three parts: identifying users, attracting users, and user characteristics. Dingdong determines its users through its service content, target user characteristics, and big data analysis. It attracts users through methods such as recipe recommendations, group buying, street stalls, and WeChat. User characteristics can be summarized in five categories of user descriptions.

Case 12

The Business Model Innovation of Yue-Life

Key Points:

Business model canvas; Business model innovation; Value creation logic of business models

Case Purpose:

Through the study of this case, students will understand the value creation logic of business models, master the tool of the business model canvas, and develop the ability to analyze business models using the value creation logic of the business model canvas.

Case Description:

1. Model 1.0

On December 12, 2012, Yue-Life was registered and established with only Li Wei as the full-time member of the management team. Liu Jun, one of the founding shareholders, did not officially join the management team. Although Yue-Life was positioned as an Internet housekeeping company, its development strategy was "offline 2C, starting with people": "offline 2C" referred to the gradual transition from offline to O2O due to resource constraints; "starting with people" meant that in order to improve service, it was necessary to first improve the service ability and professional enthusiasm of service personnel.

In 2013, the housekeeping service training room was set up with an area of only 100 square meters, able to accommodate a maximum of 80 to 100 people at a time. From 2013 to 2014, Li Wei conducted professional skills training for more than 4,000 service personnel, including service standards, service skills, service image and etiquette, communication skills, etc.

Many people asked Li Wei, "Is it worth it to provide training for 2,000 service personnel every year when only 20% of them choose to join Yue-Life?" Li Wei believed it was worth it for the following reasons. First, domestic service personnel generally lacked professionalism, so domestic service training was necessary. Second, domestic service personnel were generally considered to provide inefficient, repetitive, and low-value labor with low income levels. However, by improving their skills in domestic service, they could reduce costs, increase efficiency, and create more income. Third, there were no unified standards in the domestic service industry, and the quality and effectiveness of the service relied solely on the service personnel. Since there were no ready-made standards, it was most feasible for the company to establish and practice the standards. Fourth, the service personnel were generally older, mostly in the 40 to 50 age range. However, the trend was towards younger service personnel. By improving the knowledge and competitiveness of the service personnel through training, more young people could be attracted to join the domestic service industry.

While providing training, Yue-Life also opened its first offline service support and supply station (referred to as the store, later known as Cloud store). The store was simply decorated and divided into different areas, including a service consultation counter, storage area for equipment and materials, rest area, battery charging area, and restroom. The service consultation counter was mainly managed by the store manager, responsible for receiving orders, dispatching orders, and cashiering. The storage area was used to neatly store service utensils and materials. The rest area, battery charging area, and restroom were designed as supply stations for service personnel, where they could have free access to hot water, hot meals, air conditioning, chat, and rest. During breaks, they could also charge their batteries.

Speaking of restrooms, this was a distinctive feature of the store. Similar service stores in the market would not have their own restrooms. When the store was equipped with restrooms, service personnel within a 3-kilometer radius could use them. The primary purpose of the store was to provide basic conditions for the service personnel. Sometimes, the company would choose to rent apartments in residential areas instead of shops because it could also solve the accommodation problem for the store manager.

The operation of the store may seem simple, but not every store manager understood the original intention of setting up the store from the beginning. There was a store manager who, in order to save costs, limited the supply of purified water in the summer, resulting in a situation where service personnel had no water to drink. Upon learning about this, Li Wei immediately communicated with the store manager. In the hot summer, service personnel consume a large amount of water due to the high temperature. On average, each store consumes three barrels of water per day. As the logistical management and supply station for service personnel, if even the basic drinking water is restricted, it will inevitably affect the work enthusiasm and service quality of the service personnel.

From 2012 to 2014, Li Wei focused on training and setting up stores, concentrating on the upstream of the service supply chain. They promoted their target customers through Weibo, WeChat, and advertisements. However, during this period, Yue Housekeeper's revenue growth was slow.

2. Model 2.0

In 2014, Yue-Life's fund reached a low point, and the founders began discussing external financing. In 2015, Yue-Life received a 5 million yuan venture capital investment from Jinwei Management Fund. This was the first external financing since the establishment of Yue-Life.

After the successful external financing, Yue-Life chose to invest in the O2O field, transforming its offline store model into the O2O domestic service model of online traffic attraction and offline service output. In 2015, the "Yue-Life" App was launched, officially embarking on the Internet exploration of domestic services.

Yue-Life O2O service cloud platform linked upstream service personnel and downstream users. On the one hand, users attracted by Baidu and 58.com could browse through the platform to find specific services, including their content and prices. On the other hand, service personnel could optimize service quality through the O2O service cloud platform of Yue-Life.

During the initial focus on opening offline stores, Li Wei realized that changing and cultivating domestic service personnel and managers was the core of the development of this industry. Therefore, the Yue-Life team never stopped exploring human resources development.

The human resources development mainly focused on the training and motivation of core personnel in the management and operations team, as well as the training of grassroots personnel involved in service implementation. For the former, Yue-Life mainly provided incentives through stock options and limited partnership shares. For the latter, which had a relatively larger number of people, Yue-Life used a mechanism for selecting and utilizing key positions. After passing assessments, service personnel could improve their service ratings. Once they accumulated enough service experience, they could become partners in Yue-Life's offline stores, transitioning from service personnel to managers.

When Yue-Life entered the O2O field, the market had already experienced the most intense period of subsidies. However, subsidies seemed to be a standard practice for promoting internet products. While Yue-Life focused on the foundational development of service personnel training and assessment, competitors had already obtained a large number of users through subsidies. In the fast-paced development of the internet industry, investors also preferred projects that could achieve rapid growth. If Yue-Life only focused on human resource development without increasing the number of orders, the trained service personnel would go to other platforms with more orders, and the remaining market share would decrease.

After discussions, Yue-Life decided to start implementing strategic subsidies. The hourly service price for basic cleaning services was reduced by 10 yuan. However, for Yue-Life, the hourly service profitability decreased from 3.5 yuan to a loss of 6.5 yuan. This round of subsidies had a significant effect on Yue-Life's customer acquisition. The monthly sales volume for basic household cleaning services exceeded 10,000 orders.

3. Model 3.0

At this critical juncture, Yue-Life's management decision-making team welcomed a new member, Liu Jun, who was also one of the founding shareholders of Yue-Life. After Liu Jun took on the role of CEO, she not only put the company's internal management on track, but also found a way out for Yue-Life who was deeply involved in the O2O subsidy war.

Liu Jun believed that when big platforms merged, external capital stopped continuous injection, and subsidies gradually disappeared, it became increasingly important to control Yue-Life's cash flow and cost-benefit management. Cash flow is the fundamental condition for the survival and expansion of a company. The current development model of Yue-Life had three main flaws: First, the subsidy promotion effect was not as expected; second, the service demand from the consumer side was highly concentrated, and resource allocation efficiency needed optimization; third, the service categories were relatively single, and the service system needed improvement, unable to form a comparative advantage.

Therefore, Liu Jun's first decision after becoming CEO of Yue-Life was to cut off unprofitable businesses and stop customer acquisition subsidies. This change led to a decrease in monthly orders from over 10,000 to over 2,000, and a significant loss of service personnel due to reduced income. In order to stabilize the service personnel, Yue-Life adjusted their labor income, provided long-distance subsidies, and organized dedicated personnel to communicate with the service personnel. In the fourth month after the subsidy cancellation, the monthly orders for C-end cleaning services returned to the pre-adjustment level.

When Yue-Life discovered the imbalance in household service demand between weekdays and weekends, they decided to develop B-end business, which mainly included cleaning services for vacation rentals, hotels, apartments, and office properties. Because the service time for B-end business complemented the peak period of C-end business, Yue-Life's service personnel could be assigned to more suitable orders in most cases.

Airbnb, the global leader in vacation rentals, encountered cleaning challenges after entering China. As a result, Airbnb started looking for cleaning suppliers in China and eventually chose Yue-Life. On the Airbnb platform, hosts can book Yue-Life's cleaning services online, and Yue-Life's system will instantly receive the orders, automatically confirm the service time, and allocate service personnel. For Airbnb, this partnership with a third-party not only reduced cleaning costs by more than 30% but also provided a better experience for guests.

As Yue-Life continued to optimize cleaning service efficiency, they gradually encountered the current ceiling of the industry. The cost invested was no longer balanced with the benefits gained. How to maintain the quality of their own cleaning services while developing new single products had been a persistent problem for Liu Jun and her team.

In January 2017, Liu Jun coincidentally came into contact with a partner in the food and catering industry. He suddenly realized that there was a huge market demand in the food industry, and its replicability was very high. As a result, Yue-Life opened its first neighborhood restaurant in the Caohejing Development Zone, providing healthy meals for white-collar workers in the development zone, relying on a smoke-free central kitchen. However, due to customers' dissatisfaction with the food, the first Yue-Life restaurant failed quickly.

This failure did not discourage Liu Jun and his team. Yue-Life improved the taste of the dishes by purchasing advanced micro-kitchen equipment from Germany. They also supplied ingredients through pre-processing and standard operating procedures in a central factory, allowing chefs to focus on controlling the cooking process and finishing touches. To enhance the user experience, Yue-Life introduced facial recognition in the park canteen.

Yue-Life's customers included the First Import Expo, National Olympic Sports Center, China University of Political Science and Law, China University of Geosciences, China Institute of Metrology, Caohejing Park, Shangshi, and Bailian. Enterprise service became the entry point for Yue-Life to replicate and expand into a new city.

When considering how to effectively manage upstream service personnel, Liu Jun and his team developed the "Cloud Store" partner development model, taking inspiration from Kazuo Inamori's "Amoeba" model. "Cloud Store" was a unit established outside of the company's internal management, specifically for recruiting, training, and managing service personnel. Its predecessor was the early offline stores. "Cloud Store" partners were responsible for daily management and operations and were usually selected from experienced service personnel with high seniority, good performance, and abundant experience. Through efforts, Yue-Life's revenue grew more than 150 times in four years, and the "2C+2B, Time Sharing" model also gained recognition from investors. In 2017, Yue-Life received tens of millions of yuan of investment with a valuation of more than 200 million yuan.

4. Model 4.0

The level of competition in the domestic service industry exceeded Liu Jun's expectations. From a strategic perspective, Liu Jun analyzed consumers, service providers, and operators and found the following: On the consumer side, young people gradually became the main consumer force, and their home service needs showed clear upgrades. On the service provider side, there was a severe shortage of qualified domestic service personnel, and they lacked a strong sense of workplace fulfillment, leading to high turnover. On the operator side, domestic service companies faced challenges in managing a large service radius and operating difficulties due to providing on-site services.

To solve the above problems, consumers, it was necessary to coordinate and upgrade consumers, service providers, and operators within a single system. Therefore, in 2019, Yue-Life proposed the Butterfly Business Model, aiming to create an ccosystem where consumers, service providers, and Yue-Life could all benefit from efficiency revolution.

Liu Jun believed that the domestic service industry had low service efficiency, matching efficiency, and communication efficiency. To improve efficiency, it was essential to enhance service providers' identification with the service industry and Yue -Life. By truly understanding and cultivating service providers from the three dimensions they cared about the most, including income, growth, and respect, the stability and continuous growth of the team could be guaranteed. Yue-Life conducted in-depth analysis and design of the service provider's full career lifecycle from recruitment to training, job placement, and promotion, continuously enhancing their identification with domestic services.

With the development of the times, young people have gradually become the main consumer group in society. In an environment of rapid technological development and an accelerating pace of life, their lifestyle, habits, and other aspects underwent significant changes. Time became increasingly fragmented, and to match this change, service providers had to provide products and organizational forms that were fragmented and personalized.

Due to changes in family structures and the increased life pressures faced by young people today, they tend to outsource their household service needs. Meanwhile, we are in the era of consumer sovereignty, and consumers prefer to choose and purchase goods and services according to their own preferences and desires. In the Internet age, relying on information asymmetry to earn profits is not a sustainable direction for long-term business development. Liu Jun firmly believed that only by making consumers genuinely identify with the products or services provided by the company, truly providing convenience to consumers, could a company truly grasp the market.

Yue-Life started from three Key Points: service safety (reassurance), service convenience (worry-free), and service quality and experience (comfort). It deeply explored consumer needs and designed each key point to strive to meet consumers' comprehensive demands.

The main reason for the lack of effective connection between consumers and service providers is the lack of a trust system. Consumers believe that the actual cost of service providers is much lower than the price they pay, while service providers believe that the price paid by consumers does not match the service quality. Moreover, service providers can be divided into actual service providers and service matching platforms, and actual service providers believe that the platform's profit margin is much higher than the actual cost borne by the platform. This leads to the frequent occurrence of "cherry-picking" behavior in the service industry. In order to balance the concerns of the three parties, Yue-Life is committed to building a trust system in the service industry, continuously improving the efficiency of service providers, and reducing service costs through technological innovation and the reformation of corporate management processes.

Yue-Life's efficiency platform serves as the connector between consumers and service providers and is the core of Yue-Life's Butterfly Business Model. By utilizing Internet technology, Yue-Life has established a shared service platform, integrating social service provider resources to provide excellent service quality and experience for families and businesses, reducing communication costs between consumers, service providers, and Yue-Life, and achieving a win-win situation for all three parties. Yue-Life also established a dedicated technology research and development team, autonomously developing business systems, constantly refining the platform, and striving to maximize efficiency.

In terms of service efficiency, Yue-Life developed a team of highly educated and young service providers in the home service industry, guiding them to maintain work passion while improving work efficiency. In terms of matching efficiency, Yue-Life's automatic dispatching system included functions such as rule engine-based scoring for dispatching, priority given to high-star or high-skilled service providers, priority given to long-term regular customers, optimization of user preference data, optimization of service provider routing data, and continuous optimization of big data recommendation efficiency. In terms of communication efficiency, Yue-Life provided an open platform for service ordering through online and offline channels (WcChat, PC, App, phone), combined with 24-hour online butler and automatic background check for service providers, the enterprise endorsement of trust and zero-delay feedback, ensuring the maximization of communication efficiency between consumers and service providers, consumers and Yue-Life, and Yue-Life and service providers.

Questions:

1. Please draw the business model canvas for each stage of Yue-Life's business model iteration.

2. What kind of value creation logic do you think exists in each of the four stages of Yue-Life's business model iteration?

Case Analysis:

1. The business model canvas consists of the following elements: customer segmentation, value proposition, channel channels, key businesses, revenue sources, core resources, cost structure, important cooperation and customer relationships. From Model 1.0 to Model 4.0, Yue-Life's business model canvas has undergone changes in each stage, which can be analyzed based on these elements.

2. The logic of business model to create value is shown in the following aspects: value discovery, value matching and value acquisition. Yue-Life's value creation logic is different in each stage.

Case 13

Achieving Precise Poverty Alleviation through Social Entrepreneurship: Longyou Free-range Chicken

Key Points:

Definition of social entrepreneurship; Differences between social entrepreneurship and business entrepreneurship; Identification process and legitimacy of social entrepreneurship opportunities

Case Purpose:

Through the study of the Longyou Free-range Chicken entrepreneurship project, students will understand social entrepreneurship as a form of entrepreneurship, learn the differences between social entrepreneurship and business entrepreneurship, and understand the legitimacy strategies in the social entrepreneurship process.

Text:

1. Introduction to Longyou Chicken

Chen Yongjun has been engaged in business model design, cultural innovation, and brand design, and has accumulated a wealth of experience in company management by running an Internet company and a cultural company.

In May 2016, when Chen Yongjun accompanied his friend Hu Jingwen to visit his family in Longyou County, Zhejiang Province, he was attracted by the local Chicken in Longyou. Chen learned that although Longyou Chicken was of good quality, it was poorly marketed and local farmers were struggling to make ends meet. Seeing this, Chen wanted to change the situation and help farmers increase their income, so he started to assist in selling chickens for the farmers.

While commonly available chickens in the market are fed with feed, Longyou Chicken is different. They are free-range chickens raised in the mountains, with high egg production and good egg quality. They have been exported since 1973 and were included in the list of protected livestock and poultry genetic resources in Zhejiang Province in 2013.

Through research, Chen Yongjun found that the reason Longyou Chicken couldn't be sold well was that it was a traditional local breed without reputation outside of Longyou, and there was a limited consumer base in other areas. Additionally, most of the farming households were located in remote mountainous areas with inconvenient transportation. While free-range chickens raised in the mountains were popular among urban dwellers, it was not easy to find genuine free-range chickens. Chen Yongjun discovered that the market for free-range chickens was mixed, with many vendors falsely labeling feed-fed chickens as free-range. He believed that opening up sales channels was the key to reversing the situation, and that impoverished farmers should change their existing sales methods and take the initiative.

Due to the severe homogeneity of free-range chicken in the market, Chen named Longyou Chicken as Longyou Free-range Chicken. He set up a vertical e-commerce platform through the WeChat official account "Longyou Free-range Chicken" to connect rural specialty products with urban consumers. Afterwards, he persuaded Hu Jingwen to join the team.

On December 2, 2016, the e-commerce platform was officially launched. In order to change the previous situation of the chickens with no packaging, brand or specification, Chen and Hu set strict standards for the whole process from slaughtering to packaging, sales and logistics, thus ensuring the stability, safety and standardization of the quality of the free-range chickens. They also extensively promoted the project using their accumulated network resources, resulting in a high demand for Longyou Chicken, which was previously unsold.

2. Leading Farmers in Chicken Farming

Having achieved their initial goal, Chen and Hu could have returned to their previous lives.

However, after seeing farmers in need of help, they decided to stay and engage in chicken farming together. Their decision faced opposition and misunderstandings from their families and friends, but they did not give up despite the external negativities. In December 2017, Longyou Zongtai Agricultural Products Co., Ltd. (hereinafter referred to as Longyou Zongtai) was officially incorporated. With the vision of "everyone has something to do, every family has income," the company aimed to help farmers out of poverty and increase their income.

To dispel the farmers' doubts, the two proposed the commitment of "three exemptions and two guarantees." The "three exemptions" included providing free two-month-old mature chicks to improve chick survival rates, building free chicken coops, fences, and other supporting facilities to help farmers with preliminary preparations, and providing free access to internet connections and installing real-time IoT monitoring devices. The "two guarantees" involved signing repurchase agreements to ensure the purchase of chickens and eggs at market prices, as well as purchasing breeding insurance for Longyou Free-range Chicken.

They first convinced the retired village director to raise chickens. With the example set by the retired director, many farmers followed suit. They actively coordinated with government departments, expressing their intentions to help farmers shake off poverty. Many government officials had multiple discussions with them and conducted in-depth inspections of the "Longyou Free-range Chicken" project. They helped connect them with media resources and strongly recommended them to local poor households. With the strong promotion from the government, major mainstream media outlets such as Xinhua News Agency, CCTV, People's Daily Online, Zhejiang Satellite TV, and Zhejiang Daily all reported on Longyou Free-range Chicken.

In September 2018, the poverty alleviation model of Longyou Free-range Chicken was successfully replicated in Xuyong County, Luzhou City, Sichuan Province and Bama County, Guangxi Province. According to statistics, in 2018, the Longyou Free-range

Chicken project helped more than 700 rural households achieve prosperity through chicken farming.

The implementation of " three exemptions and two guarantees" has opened up opportunities for the Longyou Free-range Chicken project. In order to further tap into the potential of the project and help farmers become prosperous, Chen Yongjun developed the following plans.

(1) Priority for Poor Households
In order to help low-income farmers get rid of poverty in a targeted manner, Chen decided to prioritize families with disabilities, low-income families, left-behind populations in remote mountainous areas, and mountainous planting households as designated cooperative households for the Longyou Free-range Chicken project. To ensure the interests of these households and the quality of chicken farming, Chen Yongjun established unified breeding standards, greatly improving the quality and effectiveness of chicken farming for the farmers.

(2) Future Cooperation with Financial Institutions
To address the problem of farmers lacking assets and having difficulty obtaining bank loans, Chen Yongjun proposed a strategic cooperation agreement between Longyou Zongtai and Longyou Rural Commercial Bank in Quzhou. The bank provides corresponding financial loans and agricultural financial services to farmers based on the income from chicken farming.

(3) Cooperation with Economically Disadvantaged Villages
Whether the chicken breeds are genuine is the key to the long-term market dominance of Longyou Free-range Chicken. However, since Longyou Zongtai started cooperating with farmers, the breeding of chicks has always been entrusted to external sources, resulting in high cooperation costs and difficulties in ensuring quality. To address this, Chen Yongjun decided to establish a seedling breeding center that could control costs and

quality. Through investigation, Chen Yongjun found several villages in Longyou County suitable for hatching chicks. Establishing the seedling breeding center not only ensures the quality of the chicken breeds but also promotes collective income growth in these villages. Regarding profit distribution, considering the urgent need for collective income growth in the villages, Chen Yongjun chose the fastest effective method: for every healthy chick that leaves the seedling breeding center, the village collective receives a cash income of 2 yuan.

3. Flying into Thousands of Households

The success of Longyou Free-range Chicken relies on market selection and customer choices. When initially selling chickens for farmers, Chen Yongjun's target customers were urban consumers with a demand for green food and the ability to consume.

So, how could they attract consumers to buy Longyou Free-range Chicken? First, they aimed to build consumer trust in the quality of green food. By livestreaming real-time scenes of the farmers' breeding process, they deepened consumers' trust in the authenticity of Longyou Free-range Chicken and its ecological nature.

Second, they used authentic rural scenes and the living conditions of farmers to evoke consumers' emotions and their desire to change the backward rural situation. Chen Yongjun released a documentary series called "Rural Entrepreneurs" on the WeChat platform, which documented the significant changes in farmers' lives since they started breeding Longyou Free-range Chicken. Through personal testimonies and farming scenes, consumers were able to genuinely experience the impact of purchasing Longyou Free-range Chicken and its ability to help farmers generate income and improve their lives.

The corporate mission of Longyou Zongtai is "feeding a family with one chicken and supporting a college student with one egg." Longyou Free-range Chicken conveys the vision and sentiment of "everyone has something to do, every family has income" to consumers. To increase the product's visibility, Chen Yongjun developed two sales routes: online, by establishing a WeChat group for "Longyou Free-range Chicken," and offline, by creating unique experiences and inviting customers to visit the actual production site.

In 2021, the Longyou Free-range Chicken project launched the "Hundred Cities Linking Thousands of Farmers, Thousand Enterprises Connecting Thousand Villages" campaign, which accurately coincided and seamlessly integrated with Zhejiang Province's special action "Connecting a Thousand Enterprises with a Thousand Villages, Eradicating Economically Disadvantaged Villages." This event brought sustainable win-win situations for both the company and farmers.

Questions:

1. Why did Chen Yongjun launch the Longyou Free-range Chicken project?

2. How does the Longyou Free-range Chicken project differ from typical business projects?

3. How did Chen Yongjun overcome the difficulties in the initial stage of the Longyou Free-range Chicken project and eventually gain social recognition?

Case Analysis:

1. The motivation for business entrepreneurship is mostly self-centered (e.g., pursuing personal wealth), while the motivation for social entrepreneurship is mostly altruistic (e.g., pursuing social fairness). The process of identifying social entrepreneurship opportunities consists of three stages: perceiving social entrepreneurship opportunities, discovering social entrepreneurship opportunities, and creating social entrepreneurship opportunities. This question requires an analysis that combines the motivation for social entrepreneurship and the process of identifying social entrepreneurship opportunities.

2. Business entrepreneurship and social entrepreneurship are two different types of entrepreneurial activities. From the perspective of motivation, business entrepreneurship

is primarily driven by self-interest, while social entrepreneurship is primarily driven by altruism. From the perspective of the source of entrepreneurial opportunities, business entrepreneurship opportunities usually stem from unsolved market problems, while social entrepreneurship opportunities usually stem from unsolved social problems. From the perspective of entrepreneurial goals, business entrepreneurship aims to create economic value, while social entrepreneurship aims to create social value. This question can be analyzed by comparing the motivation, source of opportunities, and goals of entrepreneurship.

3. Legitimacy is crucial for the development of entrepreneurial activities. Entrepreneurial activities that possess legitimacy are more likely to obtain resources and sustained support. Since social entrepreneurship often requires innovative means to solve social problems, it also faces some challenges in legitimacy. At this point, strategies need to be adopted to promote the formation of legitimacy in social entrepreneurship. Legitimacy can be divided into regulatory legitimacy, normative legitimacy, and cognitive legitimacy. This question can be analyzed by examining the specific measures taken by the Longyou Free-range Chicken project to obtain legitimacy from these perspectives.

Case 14

Inheritance of Entrepreneurship: Hailun Piano

Key Points:

Family entrepreneurship; Inter-generational goals

Case Purpose:

This case, based on the Hailun family's entrepreneurial succession, mainly describes the process of Hailun Piano's inheritance of entrepreneurship, enabling students to understand the formation of family goals in the context of family business succession and entrepreneurship, comprehend how inter-generational family interaction promotes compatibility of inter-generational goals, and understand the role of compatibility of inter-generational goals in promoting family business succession and entrepreneurship.

Case Description:

On January 28, 2019, in the Spring Festival Gala broadcast by CCTV, more than 70 Hailun pianos and several performers selected by Hailun Piano participated in the recording of the program "I Love You China". In fact, this is not the first time that Hailun Piano received public attention. As early as 2008, Hailun Piano was selected as the piano for the Beijing Olympic series of performances and received high praise from leading European music magazine *Diapason*. Today, Hailun Piano Co., Ltd. (hereinafter referred to as Hailun Piano) has become a key national cultural export enterprise, with its product sales ranking among the top in the world. As a private enterprise, Hailun Piano has undergone a complete transformation and upgrade from scratch, from component production to complete piano production, from manufacturing industry to service industry.

1. The Industry Background and Company Status

Piano production has a history of hundreds of years abroad, but its development history in

China is not long. In recent years, the rapid economic development has promoted the popularity of piano in Chinese families. The market size of the Chinese piano industry reached 100.3 billion yuan in 2018 and 104.2 billion yuan in 2019. Among them, the market size of digital pianos has been growing, and in 2022, the market size of digital pianos in China reached 7.9 billion yuan, expected to grow to 10 billion yuan by 2025. At the same time, policies promoting the development of the piano industry have been continuously introduced to provide policy support for the development of the piano industry.

Hailun Piano was founded in 2001 and is mainly engaged in piano manufacturing, musical instrument products, automobile parts, and other businesses. It has a registered capital of 254 million yuan and is a key high-tech enterprise implementing the national Torch Program and a key cultural export enterprise. As a "China Famous Trademark," the upright pianos and grand pianos produced by Hailun Piano have been widely recognized and praised worldwide, and the company's products are sold in Europe, America, Japan, and other regions. Hailun Piano has nearly 300 piano line agents in Europe and North America, over 40 piano line agents in Japan, and over 800 piano line agents worldwide.

Education and training based on smart pianos are the emerging business of Hailun Piano, integrating online and offline art education businesses, forming new competitive advantages for Hailun Piano. In 2019, Hailun Piano collaborated with the Central Conservatory of Music and Helen Continuing Education College to develop the Hailun Smart project. The Central Conservatory of Music developed teaching materials, and Hailun Piano provided teacher training and guidance worldwide, focusing on teaching effectiveness and artistic characteristics to carry out piano teaching, ushering in a new era of art education and piano teaching.

2. Construction by the First Generation: From Hardware Components to Complete Instrument Manufacturing

Before the establishment of Hailun Piano, Chen Hailun ran a hardware accessories factory, whose main business was providing accessories to domestic piano enterprises. At that time, the piano market was mainly dominated by four major brands, namely Guangdong Pearl River, Shanghai Strauss, Liaoning Nordiska and Beijing Xinghai, and the competition was intense. Chen Hailun dreamed of bringing the factory to a new platform and turned his attention to the "engine" of the piano - the core component "Mac." This meant that the company had to upgrade its main products, improve technology and craftsmanship, and build a high-quality and high-standard production line. Talent, technology, and manufacturing tools became imminent issues. Fortunately, Beijing Xinghai Company and Austria's Wendl&Lung Company provided advanced technical support to Hailun Piano at that time. In addition, Chen Hailun also spent a huge amount of money importing advanced five-axis linkage equipment from Japan. From 2001 to 2002, Hailun Piano completed equipment upgrades. In March 2003, at the Frankfurt Exhibition in Germany, Chen Hailun showcased his "Mac" products to the world. Once exhibited, the products were sought after by foreign manufacturers. It was at this exhibition that Chen Hailun deeply realized the importance of technical personnel. Subsequently, Chen Hailun hired experts to guide his factory, even using half of Hailun Piano's annual profits to pay talent commissions.

The production transformation from component production to complete piano production was a revolution for HaiLun. Riding on the success of "Mac" development, Hailun Piano established the Piano Manufacturing Engineering Technology Research Center, investing 5% of the company's annual revenue into piano manufacturing technology research and development, and registered the "HAILUN" piano trademark, starting the development of independent brand pianos. To avoid competition with domestic established manufacturers and loss of funding sources, Chen Hailun adopted a strategy of nurturing pianos through components, selling all the produced pianos to Europe and not entering the domestic market. In 2003, the first upright piano by Hailun Piano was successfully developed. In 2004, 500 upright pianos produced by Hailun Piano were sold entirely to the European market, and in 2005, Hailun Piano abandoned the piano component business, concentrated resources on producing independent brand pianos, and developed the domestic market, selling 560 HG178 grand pianos that year. In 2019, Hailun Piano's annual sales volume reached

105,000 units, ranking fourth in the world, and was officially listed on the Shenzhen Stock Exchange in 2012.

3. Concerted Efforts of Father and Son: From Instrument Manufacturing to Smart Pianos

The development concept of "slow and steady" established by the first generation of Hailun Piano deeply influenced the goal-setting of the second generation. In 2010, Chen Hailun's only son, Chen Chaofeng, joined Hailun Piano. After joining Hailun Piano, Chen Chaofeng first rotated in the factory workshop, gaining a preliminary understanding of the entire piano production process. Then, he was responsible for IPO and external investments. Through summarization and learning, Chen Chaofeng's personal abilities improved rapidly. Since the company's listing in 2012, the development of smart pianos has been put on the agenda. In 2013, Chen Chaofeng took charge of the development of smart pianos.

Although Hailun Piano had a leading position in traditional piano manufacturing, it was still a newcomer in the field of smart technology. After the failure of cooperation with Beijing University of Posts and Telecommunications, Hailun Piano began to pursue independent research and development. On the one hand, Hailun Piano drew on advanced experiences from Europe and America and conducted in-depth exploration in areas such as audio synchronization and current noise. On the other hand, with the support of audio synchronization, it continuously improved remote music communication capabilities. The development of 4G and 5G networks made remote transmission more precise. Hailun Piano used network updates to achieve remote music synchronization transmission, meeting the sound quality requirements of smart pianos, making sound quality lossless an advantage of their smart pianos. In addition, automatic performance function became another advantage of smart pianos. When one party plays a song online, the other party can reproduce the performance of that song through the smart piano, ensuring consistent intensity and key sequence, facilitating teacher-guided learning, and also suitable for real-time remote music training. However, this technology is not yet mature. For example, in terms of performance continuity, due to the reliance on electric power for automatic performance and the heat generated by batteries, it is difficult for smart pianos to maintain accurate sound for a long time. In 2014, with the development of smart pianos, Hailun Piano established a wholly-owned subsidiary, "Beijing Hailun Network Information Technology Co., Ltd.," to provide information technology support for the parent company.

4. Second Generation Taking the Lead: From Smart Pianos to Training Schools

In 2014, Chen Chaofeng founded Hailun Art Education Investment Co., Ltd. to study the art education industry of Hailun piano from manufacturing to services. Chen Chaofeng and his father believed that there was still a gap in China's art education and training market. Smart pianos could not only serve as convenient entertainment but also be used for piano teaching. Therefore, Hailun Piano established a music training school and entered the art education market. The gap in China's art enlightenment education market had given the smart pianos a place.

The smart piano laid the foundation for Hailun Piano's education and training. Chen Chaofeng's team developed an App that enabled one-to-many teaching and training. It not only reduced the cost of parents, but also enabled children to communicate with each other in the learning process. The App also used animations to stimulate children's learning interests. Hailun Piano provided corrective guidance to children through key indicator lights, and offered personalized tutoring through the software. Hailun Piano has also been actively designing its own curriculum, hiring professors from Beijing Normal University to guide the design of the curriculum, and applying it to the software of online teaching. Piano classrooms, music training schools and intelligence training schools were also gradually established. Hailun Piano also cooperated with Ningbo University to take the lead in establishing a pilot music school, and successfully signed a contract with the Central Conservatory of Music to jointly develop curriculum content.

The efforts of two generations of the Hailun family have propelled Hailun Piano from a small piano component factory to a leading company in the industry. In the process of development, Hailun Piano not only achieved the transformation and development of the enterprise but also successfully completed family succession. The joint management of father and son enabled a smooth transition between two generations, and the second generation of the family managed to grow into an excellent successor through his entrepreneurial experience.

Questions:

1. What diverse entrepreneurial goals emerged within the family business during inter-generational succession? Who are the entities setting the goals?

2. How did the interaction between two generations of family leaders affect the compatibility of diversified family business goals?

3. Why could the compatibility of goals between two generations of leaders promote the transformation of family businesses during succession?

Case Analysis:

1. A family business is a business entity jointly led by two generations of leaders, and their goals undergo changes during intergenerational succession. The leaders are the entities setting the goals, and understanding the differences in motivation for goal-setting among different entities can help family businesses understand the diversity of goals.

2. The compatibility of goals in family businesses proceeds in sync with business development and family succession, and inter-generational interaction plays an important role in adjusting the motivation of family members. It is recommended to analyze the role of inter-generational interaction in the process of goal compatibility using family science theory and social emotional wealth theory.

3. The transformation of traditional businesses is a process of gradually transferring power

from the first generation of leaders, as well as a demonstration of the entrepreneurial capabilities of the second generation of leaders. In family businesses, the demonstration of the second generation's entrepreneurial capabilities needs to be achieved with the cooperation of the first generation of leaders. The goal theory can be used to analyze how the inheritance goals and entrepreneurial goals can be achieved in the inter-generational context.